John Michael Talbot

Francis *of* Assisi's Sermon on the Mount

Lessons from *The Admonitions*

PARACLETE PRESS
Brewster, Massachusetts

2019 First Printing

Francis of Assisi's Sermon on the Mount: Lessons from The Admonitions

Copyright © 2019 by John Michael Talbot

ISBN 978-1-64060-172-7

Library of Congress Cataloging-in-Publication Data
Names: Talbot, John Michael, author.
Title: Francis of Assisi's Sermon on the mount : lessons from the Admonitions / John Michael Talbot.
Description: Brewster, MA : Paraclete Press, Inc., 2019.
Identifiers: LCCN 2019002628 | ISBN 9781640601727 (trade paper)
Subjects: LCSH: Francis, of Assisi, Saint, 1182-1226. Admonitiones. | Sermon on the mount. | Meditations–Early works to 1800. | Spiritual life—Catholic Church—Early works to 1800.
Classification: LCC BX2179.F643 T35 2019 | DDC 248.4/82—dc23
LC record available at https://lccn.loc.gov/2019002628

10 9 8 7 6 5 4 3 2 1

Published by Paraclete Press
Brewster, Massachusetts www.paracletepress.com

Printed in the United States of America

Contents

Introduction

We live in troubled times. We are experiencing polarization, anger, and even violence in the United States, and across the world. Many people feel that we are careening out of control. But God is still in control. It is important to reach deep into our Catholic Christian heritage in a way that speaks to all people to bring clarity and peace. St. Francis of Assisi is one of the great saints who somehow reaches across all divides, touches hearts and souls, and brings spiritual peace.

In a way, the Admonitions are St. Francis's Beatitudes or Sermon on the Mount. They get to his very heart, and they promise blessings throughout. But they also require great sacrifice of the old self to realize! In Scripture, a blessing is a happiness that rises above the ups and downs of daily life. For the Franciscans, they require rising above the ups and downs of life in a new religious, or consecrated, community. Leaders might be good or bad. Members might be great saints, or sinners. In Francis's time, the community was still very young, so it was far from stable. To persevere required a great faithfulness to the vision of Christ. This was faith that looked beyond the ups and downs of daily life to the fulfillment of that vision of Francis to renew a church in terrible need of reform and revival.

We live in similar times today. We see the greatest number of civilian casualties of war, and oppression of the many by the few. Poverty is on the rise, and the gap between rich and poor increases as the once hoped for rise of the middle class shrinks away. Polarization is rampant in the political and social realms as many once-Christian cultures degenerate into the confusion of a godless, secularist ideology unlike anything the world has ever seen.

In the Middle East, and in parts of Asia and Africa, we face the battle between radical Islamists and Christians where there once was mutual toleration. Many Christians are being martyred, and churches are being burned. In the Far East, Hindu nationalism is seeing a similar persecution of Christians, and Communism in some nations continues to persecute Christians in an alarming way.

The Catholic Church, and all churches and faith communities, especially in the West, are struggling to exist and evangelize amid secularism. Some fall back to an entrenched ultra-conservatism; others try a radical progressivism that too easily does away with essentials of the faith. Meanwhile, life in the average parish is exceedingly difficult, though millions continue to at least receive the basic sacramental graces. We have all heard of the sex scandals rocking the churches. They are the worst we have seen in centuries, but they are not the first, nor will they be the last.

Francis lived in similar times. He was told, "Francis, go repair my house, for as you can see, it is falling to ruin." In a church rife with sexual immorality and financial scandals among the bishops and clergy, he began to rebuild. He reformed them through radically following Jesus in humility and purity. He became a radical disciple of Jesus. And because he was such a true disciple, he was able to make disciples of both laity and clergy alike.

Most experts agree that the Admonitions had their beginnings in short teachings St. Francis would provide for his spiritual brothers when they gathered for large community meetings. These teachings were then written down and compiled, for the first time, after Francis's death. As you will soon see, they address very real, common problems, and this means they were intended to be put into practice by the friars. As in, first, listen—then, go do!

I love the stories of the earliest Franciscans, as many of you surely do. *The Little Flowers of Saint Francis*, for instance, is among the most beautiful books in all Christian history. But the Admonitions are different. One prominent Franciscan historian has emphasized that, after studying the Admonitions of the saint, one begins to look at those early friars as just ordinary Christians in the process of conversion (conversion is a lifelong process!):

> Since Francis hardly directs his words of admonition against theoretical trespasses but seeks to correct real and actual abuses in the communal life of his friars, the Admonitions, in their own way, show that the first Franciscan generation is not to be glorified unduly.[1]

We are to be the Francises of our time! We do well to study his life and teachings. May we all radically follow Jesus Christ in profound humility. Then from that humble but confident faith can we do our part in reforming our church today. St. Francis wrote these Admonitions to address struggles his friars, or spiritual brothers, were experiencing. They are applicable to anyone seeking to follow Jesus in a deeper way.

I have written two bigger books on St. Francis, *Reflections on St. Francis* and *The Lessons of St. Francis*. In this third one, I attempt to bring these relatively little-known writings of his to bear on our contemporary situation. Much of my commentary is based on my own experience as a monastic and a Franciscan.

I cherish my memories of first encounters with Franciscan sources. I used to walk the prayer paths at Alverna Franciscan Center in Indianapolis for hours with a Bible and an *Omnibus of Sources* in a tote bag. I'd sit by the creek on some rocks, or under the shade of huge trees, and read prayerfully. Later, I would do the same in the hermitage I built by the creek behind

[1] Kajetan Esser, *Origins of the Franciscan Order* (Chicago: Franciscan Herald Press, 1970), 269.

a Marian shrine. In those idyllic settings, the Admonitions settled deep in my soul.

The Admonitions are at once some of the most beautiful, and troubling, of Francis's writings. Some folks love them for their challenging nature. Some folks of more modern sensibilities are repulsed by that same challenging nature! Most who are repulsed by them would also be repulsed by an initial read of the Desert Fathers and Mothers, or much of the monastic tradition in general. Some of the themes in these Admonitions—they are aptly named!—can feel harsh to people who love St. Francis according to the popular understanding of him—for how he loved animals and people. But, as we'll see, there is more to Francis than meets the eye.

My hope and purpose is to get beyond some of the cultural differences in faith and devotion, and get down to the universal lessons and applications in the Admonitions for today. They comprise twenty-eight teachings in total.

For me, they are a combination of the sayings of the Desert Fathers and *The Imitation of Christ*. They have the earthy pithiness of the Desert Fathers, yet they are distinctly Western in their theology and devotion. In just a few words entire spiritual issues are addressed. Though very loving, they cut to the heart of the matter. They are no-nonsense. They cut to the chase! Most of their content can be found in earlier monastic sources, but Francis puts it together in his own distinct way, unique to his own culture, time, and development in the church.

The Admonitions range in length from several paragraphs to just two lines. They cover everything from sacramental theology of the Eucharist, to communal issues of consecrated life, to very private aspects of devotion and faith. They challenge much of the religious status quo of his day, and of ours. They will challenge us!

There is a certain repetition of themes throughout. This can be boring, but stay with St. Francis, and with me. When we understand the central premise of dying with Christ through his cross to rise a new person in him, any repetitions begin to make sense. They are clear road signs to the destination on our spiritual journey in Christ. In all that follows, I hope and pray that you are as challenged and encouraged by these writings of St. Francis as I have been.

Admonition 1
The Blessed Sacrament

⟪◌ ST. FRANCIS WROTE:

"Jesus said to him, 'I am the way, and the truth, and the life; no one comes to the Father, but by me. If you had known me, you would have known my Father also; henceforth you know him and have seen him.' Philip said to him, 'Lord, show us the Father, and we shall be satisfied.' Jesus said to him, 'Have I been with you so long, and yet you do not know me, Philip? He who has seen me has seen the Father; how can you say, "Show us the Father"?'" (John 14:6–9).

Sacred Scripture tells us that the Father dwells in "unapproachable light" (1 Tim. 6:16) and that "God is spirit" (John 4:24), and St. John adds, "No one has ever seen God" (1:18). "It is the spirit that gives life, the flesh is of no avail; the words that I have spoken to you are spirit and life" (John 6:63). But God the Son is equal to the Father, and so he too can be seen only in the same way as the Father and the Holy Spirit.

That is why all those were condemned who saw our Lord Jesus Christ in his humanity but did not see or believe in spirit in his divinity, that he was the true Son of God. In the same way now, all those are damned who see the sacrament of the body of Christ that is consecrated on the altar in the form of bread and wine by the words of our Lord in the hands of the priest, and do not see or believe in spirit and in God that this is really the most holy body and blood of our Lord Jesus Christ. It is the Most High himself who has told us, "Take, eat; this is my body. . . . For this is my blood of the covenant, which is poured out for many for the forgiveness of sins" (Matt. 26:26, 28). And, "He who eats my flesh and drinks my blood has eternal life, and I will raise him up at the last day" (John 6:54).

So it is really the Spirit of God who dwells in his faithful who receive the most holy body and blood of our Lord. Anyone who does not have this Spirit and presumes to receive him "eat and drink judgment against themselves" (1 Cor. 11:29). And so we may ask in the words of Scripture, "How long will you be dull of heart?" (Ps. 4:3 Douay-Rheims). Why do you refuse to recognize the truth and believe in the Son of God? Every day he humbles himself just as he did when he came from his heavenly throne into the Virgin's womb; every day he comes to us and lets us see him in abjection, when he descends from the bosom of the Father into the hands of the priest at the altar. He shows himself to us in this sacred bread just as he once appeared to his apostles in real flesh. With their own eyes they saw only his flesh, but they believed that he was God, because they contemplated him with the eyes of the spirit. We, too, with our own eyes see only bread and wine, but we must see further and firmly believe that this is his most holy body and blood, living and true. In this way, our Lord remains continually with his followers, as he promised, "Behold, I am with you all days, even unto the consummation of the world" (Matt. 28:20).

———————————————————————

This is the lengthiest and probably most difficult of the Admonitions for most Christians today. Of all the saints and religious founders and leaders in the history of our faith, St. Francis remains the most beloved. Still, we don't often associate him with a teaching such as this. Yet, for Catholics, Orthodox, and other Eucharistic-based Christians, the subject of this Admonition remains at the heart of our common worship and communion with Jesus. It brings up a wide array of topics.

I must admit, this Admonition left me a bit cold at the beginning of my journey into the Catholic Church, and I would often skip over it. Not that I didn't love the Eucharist. I did. But it seemed off-putting to non-Catholics who loved St. Francis. Now, in later years, it seems perfect at the beginning. My love for the Eucharist has grown over the decades, and I realize that, while Jesus devoted precious little time to it, the early church considered it the greatest sacramental way to profess the essential truths of Jesus Christ, and to bring his real incarnational presence into each day. It should also be remembered that Francis was teaching a Catholic culture and trying to bring it back to a personal encounter with Jesus in the power of the Holy Spirit. So it is a perfect place for him to start. We will start there as well.

The religious world of Italy in the time of St. Francis was confronted with challenges. There had been an explosion of new communities around 150 years or so before Francis lived, in the eleventh century. These were based on a return to monastic basics of contemplative prayer, solitude, and an enlivened sense of living the gospel. This predated and affected the time of Francis. By the time of Francis there were a great number of new communities and itinerant preachers trying to live the gospel as purely and radically as possible. Some of these communities were orthodox, and some were not.

One such community was the Cathars. They were a neo-Manichaean group that lived in extreme poverty. Like proponents of Manichaeism before them, they were Gnostics based on an erroneous dualistic belief that flesh was evil and spirit was good. Another group was the Poor Men of Lyons, also known as the Waldensians. Some of them remained faithful to the church, and some did not. Those who broke away from the Catholic Church believed so strongly in the purity of the gospel that they broke from the ordained priesthood of the Catholic Church and claimed that only personal holiness gave one the authority to celebrate the Lord's Supper. Of course, this predated the Protestant Reformation, and led to a splintering of the church since everyone had their own opinion about what is really holy, or not.

In response to both of these groups, the Cathars and the Waldensians, St. Francis was clear and insistent in his obedience to the Catholic Church. He believed in the ancient and developing apostolic teaching of the early church. Though often abused on a subjective level by the personal lives of the clergy, it was still correctly maintained and encouraged correctly on the objective level by the clergy. Francis held fast to that gospel tradition as it had been passed on from the beginnings of the church to his current time.

The early church had to face Manichaean and Gnostic factions. The Eucharist was a strong affirmation of the incarnation and the hypostatic union of Jesus. The church maintained a balance between the humanity and the divinity of Christ. Jesus was completely God and human in his body, soul, and spirit. Manichaeans believed that flesh and matter were evil and only spirit was good—which radically affected their full understanding of Jesus. They ended up denying the Incarnation, which literally means, "in meat, or flesh." Consequently, they also denied Christ's full humanity, which means that they only accepted his divinity. Docetists, similarly, believed that Jesus only "seemed" human. This fouled up their understanding of the hypostatic union, or the balanced union of the human and divine in Christ.

The church affirmed these things in the celebration of the Eucharist. If you believe in the Real Presence under the appearance of bread and wine, then this is based on the belief in the goodness of spirit and matter, the Incarnation, and the hypostatic union. Without these, the traditional belief in the Eucharist does not make any sense. Conversely, the belief in the Eucharist confirms and strengthens these things.

Related to this is the traditional belief that each human being is composed of a body and a soul, material and spiritual. St. Paul teaches that the human being is composed of "spirit and soul and body" (1 Thess. 5:23). This tripartite definition has also been used by monastic and Eastern Christian fathers. The body includes the senses and the chemical or material makeup of our emotions and thoughts. The spiritual mind is the soul. The spirit is the deepest part of our being and is expressed through pure spiritual intuition. Through sin we have reversed the order of priority and placed the body and senses first, and this wreaks havoc on the emotions and thoughts, with the spirit being forgotten entirely. Through Christ this order is set right, with the spirit being first, facilitated by the thoughts; thoughts direct the emotions, which are housed in the senses of the body. This understanding has radical effects on understanding why we die and are raised up in Jesus Christ.

This division is not meant to compartmentalize or fracture the human being; it is meant to define us and help us understand the various parts of who we are. The priority of the spirit is in no way interpreted as a belittlement of the thoughts, emotions, and senses. Nor does it mean that they are not a real part of who we are as creatures of God created in God's image and likeness. Such an interpretation would be a mistake.

The Eucharist is an affirmation of the goodness of the senses, and of the material world. It is not only the spirit and the spiritual world that is good. God created the entire world and pronounced it "good." It is only through our abuse of ourselves and of creation through sin that the world and the flesh become a hindrance and an obstacle to life with God. The Eucharist is a confirmation of this understanding, and an aid to overcoming any abuses or weaknesses on our part.

I come from the Jesus Movement and the Catholic Charismatic Renewal. Along with the Franciscan and monastic traditions, the Charismatic Renewal was most helpful in greeting me as I entered the church. In renewal, there have sometimes been discussions about whether you need liturgy and sacraments if you have the anointing of the Spirit of God. Francis would disagree with any suggestion of a conflict between these. Rather than saying that we need to do away with liturgy because some liturgies are bad, Francis would recommend renewing liturgy and the sacraments. In other words, the liturgy and sacraments, especially the Eucharist, already have the power of the Holy Spirit within. The Real Presence of Jesus as the body, blood, soul, and divinity of Christ is confected through the Word of God prayed by the ordained priestly minister of the church. But it is up to us to fully unlock that power through lively faith.

The sacraments symbolize and effect grace. They symbolize the faith already present in a believer. They also cause that faith to grow stronger. We should not abominate them by approaching them without faith. Even minimal faith can be strengthened through well-intentioned and active participation. My deceased spiritual father, Fr. Martin Wolter, OFM, taught me that the renewal of the liturgy is like freeze-dried coffee! The coffee is already in the granules. But it takes water to release them into at least a minimally drinkable cup of coffee. The same is true with liturgy and sacraments. If we approach them with faith, and the power of the Spirit in our lives, they symbolize that faith and Spirit, and cause them to grow even stronger. We release the power of the sacraments in our life, and that power is life-changing for those who experience it.

With the eyes of the Spirit, and with the gift of faith, St. Francis could see Jesus present under the appearance of bread and wine in the Eucharist. The same could be said about the way he saw Jesus in others. Francis was able to see Jesus in the leper. He was told to embrace the one he was most afraid of, and turned off by, and he found the real presence of Jesus in that person. St. Mother Teresa said the same about the poorest of the poor, and the dying. But it is true of all people.

Who are the lepers in our lives? Who are we most afraid of, or turned off by? It is only by embracing them that we find Jesus in everyone. Who are the poor, the sick, and the dying? The poor are not an ideal where we find romantic notions about our own "ministry." The poor are real people, like you and me, who are often born into poverty, or who find themselves there through a series of bad consequences. They say that the average American is only about ninety days from the street if things go badly for them. First goes the job, then the house, then the spouse, the family, the car. There are many ex-doctors and ex-lawyers living on the street.

Anyone who has done work with the poor will be the first to tell you that poverty stinks, figuratively as well as physically. The same is true for the seriously ill and dying. It is not pretty, or immediately fulfilling, to work with these people. It is tough, and it requires the anointing of the Spirit and real faith to persevere in that ministry. But those who do persevere find the real presence of Jesus there. And it is not just the literally poor, sick, and dying that challenge us. Sometimes we can find them among the middle class, and especially among the wealthy. Mother Teresa said that we, the wealthiest nation on earth, are probably, in reality, the poorest nation on earth. This is because of our spiritual poverty, sickness, and death.

In concerts, I often perform a song called "St. Teresa's Prayer." In it are the words "Christ has no body, now, but yours. No hands, no feet on earth, but yours." I have the audience hold hands and meditate on first receiving Jesus from all those around them, the good as well as the bad. I believe that only when we can receive him from everyone we meet can we begin to really give him without it lapsing into religious self-righteousness in the name of evangelization.

All are created in the image of God. All have sinned and fallen short of the glory of God. St. Bonaventure says that our soul is like a mirror created to reflect the beautiful image of God. Though this mirror has been covered up by sin, it is always there just waiting to be uncovered by the love of God. Once that happens, then the mirror can reflect the image of God once more. So, no one is without that image deep in their being. When we look with the eyes of faith, and the eyes of the Spirit, we can see that image there, regardless of whether they can. When we can see it, then we treat them as we would treat Jesus. This, in turn, calls the image of Jesus in them to the surface, and they begin to experience him in their own life as a personal love relationship.

Can we find Jesus in others? We must find him in everyone, those we like and those we do not, before we can really give him to others. Only then will we be able to say with St. Francis what he says in this first, tough Admonition:

> We, too, with our own eyes see only bread and wine, but we must see further and firmly believe that this is his most holy body and blood, living and true. In this way, our Lord remains continually with [us].

Admonition 2
The Evil of Self-Will

〰️ ST. FRANCIS WROTE:

"The LORD God commanded the man, saying, 'You may freely eat of every tree of the garden; but of the tree of the knowledge of good and evil you shall not eat, for in the day that you eat of it you shall die'" (Gen. 2:16–17). Adam could then eat his fill of all the trees in the Garden, and as long as he did not act against obedience, he did not sin. A person eats of the tree that brings knowledge of good when he claims that his good will comes from himself alone and prides himself on the good that God says and does in him. And so, at the devil's prompting and by transgressing God's command, the fruit becomes for him the fruit that brings knowledge of evil, and it is only right that he should pay the penalty.

Self-will is not considered very relevant today. We are usually more concerned with self-affirmation. For many, self-will seems not such a bad thing. We've lost something essentially deep and beautiful, which is the foundation of St. Francis's second Admonition.

The Rule of St. Benedict says in the prologue: "Listen, O my son, to the teachings of your master, and turn to them with the ear of your heart. Willingly accept the advice of a devoted father and put it into action. Thus you will return by the labor of obedience to the one from whom you drifted through the inertia of disobedience. Now then I address my words to you: whoever is willing to renounce self-will, and take up the powerful and shining weapons of obedience to fight for the Lord Christ, the true king."

This builds on the biblical tradition of both Christ and St. Paul. Paul says to the Romans, "We know that our old self was crucified with him so that the sinful body might be destroyed, and we might no longer be enslaved to sin. For he who has died is freed from sin. But if we have died with Christ, we believe that we shall also live with him" (Rom. 6:6–8). Jesus says, "If any man would come after me, let him deny himself and take up his cross and follow me. For whoever would save his life will lose it, and whoever loses his life for my sake will find it." (Matt. 16:24–25). Francis's treatment of self-will follows in this scriptural and monastic tradition.

Other religions like Buddhism deny the eternal reality of the individual self, or human soul. They believe in *anatman*, or "no soul." They see the self as having value only as a phenomenal reality that is impermanent. I'm oversimplifying, of course, but there is a resonance with Christian monastic teaching there. Buddhism has many positive things to offer people of all faiths on the human and psychological level, and Buddhists, too, raise the question of the place and value of the human self.

The Christian view is not to actually deny the self, but to see it as displaced. This is closely related to the ego. Ego simply means "self." Some people think, to be good Christians, we should get rid of our egos completely. This is neither practical nor healthy. Plus, it is just plain impossible! Without an ego or self, we would have no sense of existence. We would be like zombies in a strange land. It is not the existence of the ego that is at issue. It is how we have allowed it to operate.

This is always something I have struggled with. I have wanted to let go of my old self, and be born again as a new person in Jesus. I experienced this in the Jesus Movement and in Charismatic Renewal. When I became a Catholic, and embraced a deeper Franciscan and monastic life, my old ego and obsessed self kept creeping back in, simply refusing to leave! Even more insidiously, my old self learned to hide under my new religious lingo and culture, which existed to help me extirpate it from my self-obsessed patterns of living in the first place.

It was only after founding an integrated monastic community, and trying to lead it for a decade, that my old self-will simply got beaten out of me through the day in, day out realities of undertaking this challenge. At the beginning we attracted folks of all sorts. No matter what I suggested or tried to implement as a calling I thought I had received from God, I was often subtly or outright resisted anytime something cut into the individualism of those who said they wanted to follow the same call. Later we implemented better vocation discernment, but this still occurred subtly. This is fairly normal in forming new monastic members. So I learned that regardless of my titles as "Founder," "Spiritual Father," or "General Minister," many folks ended up resisting, and some ended up doing what they wanted to do anyway. Many simply left. While I stayed, and did so joyfully, this repeating process simply wore me out. Rather than blaming others for their problems, this brought me face-to-face with my own ego attachment to teaching my way of letting go of ego attachment! The problem was with me, not them. Consequently, the ordinary ups and downs of founding and leading a new community eventually knocked the stuffing out of me. My ego and self-will lay in shatters all around me like a rag doll that had got its stuffing knocked out.

Ironically, it was only after that took place that I found out who I really was in Christ. I went into a prolonged period of solitude and came out more humbled though a naked encounter with God and my real self, and more confident in the grace of God. I wouldn't dare say that this process is anywhere complete in my life. I'm still an egotist. But, somehow, I have at least glimpsed something of what is real in my life in Christ, not to mention in my leadership, reflected and inspired by the Franciscan and monastic traditions.

We often misunderstand our makeup as human beings. Sometimes we think that we are our senses, emotions, or thoughts. While we have these, they are not our deepest self; they are realities that constantly change, evolve, and grow. Praise God, some aspects of these things will not be with me for eternity!

There has been much debate and confusion about the difference between the soul and the spirit. Both help compose a spiritual element to the human being. It is a mistake to take these as strict scientific anthropologies. What we should take away is that we are spiritual, intellectual, emotional, and physical beings. Nor can we artificially separate one aspect from the other. We are an integrated whole of all our parts. That's why, unlike many other religions and philosophies, we believe in a resurrection of the body. Like Jesus before us, that body will be much more expanded from the dimensions we are currently limited to through sin. But we will have a glorified body, as well as a spirit and soul.

The tripartite explanation of the human being sees the body as the physical, chemical, and electrical aspects of our senses, emotions, and thoughts. The soul is the spiritual mind. The spirit is the deepest intuition of the human being—it builds on senses, emotions, and thoughts, but is beyond them all. The spirit is the deepest and most primary part of us. The soul is the spiritual cognition and enthusiasm of the spirit. The body is the house for the soul and the spirit. We need them all to be fully human. (This does not mean that people who are not spiritually awakened are less human, only that they have yet to realize their own potential as beings created by God, and fully redeemed in Jesus Christ.)

The problem is that we have often got this turned upside down. Most of us function primarily from the perspective of the senses of the body. We complain that we are too hot or too cold, hungry or thirsty, and so on. When we don't get the sensual gratification we demand, our emotions are upset, our thoughts are clouded. The spirit gets covered up entirely as if it has fallen asleep. So, our "self"-awareness is incomplete at best. Often it is false.

When our deepest self is displaced and forgotten, we begin trying to find our identity in the outer things of body and soul that were intended only to facilitate the deeper things of the spirit. This is where the false self, the ego, or the self-will comes into play. Since we mistakenly place so much of our identity in our sense, emotions, or thoughts, when we do not get what we want we become upset. To cover up the fact that we often get hurt by others when we do not get our way, or what we want, we develop a false self as a protection against such hurt. This is where egoism manifests itself. Usually behind every seeming egotist is a hurt child of God who has gotten confused about who they really are.

In a sense, this is what St. Francis is saying. For him, self-will is just the human person trying to operate separately from God. The Genesis story of the Fall is the perfect biblical example of this. As was true for Adam and Eve in the Garden, God is everywhere, all knowing, and all powerful. All he asks is for us to cooperate with his loving plan.

The tried-and-true cure for this displaced ego, this self-will, is obedience. And obedience to God simply means listening deeply. The channels for God's voice come through the Scripture and apostolic tradition of the church, and the spiritual leaders God has placed in our lives. We must listen to

God directly, and through his mediated authority on earth. All of this is a gift of divine love for us. When we listen carefully, we cannot help responding, and responding promptly, without hesitation, and with great love to the One who is love.

Are we willing to really let go of our false identity? It takes great courage to do so. But God is not out to kill us. He has only our best interest at heart. He wants to restore the peace and order to our life that he originally planned for us, and every human being. To let go takes great trust in this love. But the rewards are a restoration of our full humanity in a way that is nothing short of divine.

Admonition 3
Perfect and Imperfect Obedience

⤳ ST. FRANCIS WROTE:

Our Lord tells us in the Gospel, "Whoever of you does not renounce all that he has cannot be my disciple" (Lk. 14:33), and, "For whoever would save his life will lose it" (Lk. 9:24). A person takes leave of all that he possesses, and loses both his body and his life, when he gives himself up completely to obedience in the hands of his [community or church] superior. Any good he says or does, which he knows is not against the will of his superior, is true obedience.

(Admonition 3, part one)

With this Admonition, St. Francis begins to explain in some detail, and also with some real sophistication, the concept of religious obedience. He gets to the heart of the topic in a challenging, balanced way. We will take it in three parts.

If you ask the average informed person what the key element of St. Francis of Assisi's spirituality is, they would probably say, *poverty*. Many people still see him as "the birdbath saint." While Francis most certainly loved gospel poverty, and while he is the patron saint of ecology, neither answer would really be fully correct. Scholars, like the esteemed Kajetan Esser, OFM, say that Francis's key characteristic was his obedience. This Admonition highlights this. It says that the highest form of poverty is obedience. It is easy to be poor outwardly when we are choosing our own poverty; it is much more difficult when we are asked to sacrifice our unhealthy self-will by a spiritual leader who will hold us accountable to keep us honest with ourselves and with others. Francis says that this is the greatest poverty.

The root meaning of obedience is "to listen." When we are obedient we learn to silence our opinions and desires to really hear what others have to say. Most importantly, we learn to silence the displaced ego that so often generated our own opinions and desires. When we let go of displaced ego, then we can more easily be silent. We can be obedient.

To be silent usually means slowing down. It means stillness. This is called *hesychia*, or "sacred stillness," in the Christian East. So the listening of obedience is intimately connected with both silence and stillness. In Scripture, St. Paul uses the word *hesychia* when he encourages his readers to "aspire to live *quietly*, to mind your own affairs, and to work with your hands, as we charged you; so that you may command the respect of outsiders, and be dependent on nobody" (1 Thess. 4:11–12).

There are many liturgies and devotions that can help us with this. They all bring us into a prayer place, slow us down, and focus our minds and hearts on the sacred. For Christians, they are meant to focus us on Jesus. Eventually we pass beyond ideas and forms into pure contemplation. This is a place of complete letting go of ego and pride, and allows us to really listen, to be obedient.

Personally, I have found that sitting quietly in a still and stable posture without fidgeting, slowing, and deepening my breathing, and cleaving the name of Jesus to my breath, are most effective. This is taught most beautifully through the Jesus Prayer. I have written a book devoted to the Jesus Prayer. The main thing is to breathe in the complete reality of Jesus, the church, and our community or ministry intuitively beyond words and ideas. Then breathe out anything keeping us from a complete communion with Jesus and one another.

The word for "Spirit" and "spirit" is *pneuma*, which simply means, air, wind, and breath—specifically, the breath of a rational creature. This is one reason Jesus "breathed on them, and said to them, 'Receive the Holy Spirit'" (John 20:22). The Holy Spirit also came as a strong driving wind at Pentecost (Acts 2). We are told to "pray without ceasing" (1 Thess. 5:16). One thing we do without ceasing is to breathe! So with each breath we can unite ourselves to the Spirit and person of Jesus Christ.

It is important to first learn the correct teaching about these things. But, then, in the actual practice of them we must get to the point of going beyond the practice into pure intuition. In other words, we pray with every breath, and as we do we breathe in the fullness of our faith. This takes us into both deep repentance and awe and wonder. These are filling breaths!

Then we empty our breath. We let go of all our ego and pride, of all that is not in union with Jesus, the church, or our community or ministry with each breath out. For most people, this is an experience of complete release, physically, emotionally, and mentally. Then the deeper spirit emerges in God's Spirit. This last stage is most powerful in giving us the mechanics of meditation. Then it ceases to just be an ideal we strive for but never realize.

In our monastic community, we follow an ancient custom when receiving a person's commitments to God within the community. While someone pronounces their vows, they kneel and bring their hands together in prayer in traditional, Catholic fashion. The spiritual father or mother, or elder brother or sister, encloses their praying hands in the praying hands of the one who has come. When the vows are pronounced, the person says that they make them "into the hands" of the spiritual leader receiving them. This is a powerful symbol for everyone. It symbolizes a person's really letting go and letting God guide them through the direction of their chosen community and its leaders. A person is never forced into this. They take this action of their own free will. They renounce their self-will for the sake of God's greater will as found through that same community and leadership.

For the leaders, as they enclose the renunciant's hands within their own, they must hold them gently. The renunciant's hands must be fully enclosed, because it symbolizes the complete letting go on the part of the one making their commitment, but they must be held with great love and great care. I am always very moved by this when I receive the commitments of new members in the Brothers and Sisters of Charity at Little Portion Hermitage.

But then, of course, real obedience is more than just listening and symbolic gestures. It is an action! I am reminded of the story of the monk who heard the sound of the signal for community prayer and left his work of copying manuscripts immediately to answer the call. He dropped his pen in the middle of writing a word. He didn't hesitate, or rationalize, thinking, *I'll just finish this word, or line, paragraph, or thought, and then answer the call.* No, he went right away. While this story might sound irrational to modern ears, it demonstrates that real obedience is not only listening, but action, and immediate action at that!

Chapter 5 of the Rule of Benedict illustrates the point as well. It says, "The first step of humility is unhesitating obedience, which comes naturally to those who cherish Christ above all. Because of the holy service they have professed, or because of dread of hell and for the glory of everlasting life, they carry out the superior's order as promptly as if the command came from God himself." It goes on, "The Lord says of men like this: No sooner did he hear than he obeyed me; again, he tells teachers: Whoever listens to you, listens to me. Such people as these immediately put aside their own concerns, abandon their own will, and lay down whatever they have in hand, leaving it unfinished. With the ready step of obedience, they follow the voice of authority in their actions. Almost at the same moment, then, as the master gives the instruction the disciple quickly puts it into practice in the fear of God; and both actions together are swiftly completed as one."

This obedience is not mere military or external obedience. It is done for the love of God, and leaves no room for an inwardly grumbling spirit. The Rule continues, "It is love that impels them to pursue everlasting life; therefore, they are eager to take the narrow road of which the Lord says: Narrow is the road that leads to life (Matt 7:14). They no longer live by their own judgment, giving in to their whims and appetites; rather they walk according to another's decisions and directions, choosing to live in monasteries and to have an abbot over them."

Such immediate obedience can only be done when we let go of our ego and pride, and do everything for God, and God alone. We don't always do this because we agree, or even like and respect the person of the superior, though we hope that superiors do their best to be loved rather than feared. We do it because we deeply love God.

Are we willing to really let go and let God? Are we willing to do this by trusting others? Entering into a relationship with a community and its leaders is a way to intentionally and formally enter into this mystery. It is a mystery that brings life when done rightly. If done with reservation, or without letting go of ego and pride, it only leads to frustration and anger. Furthermore, if the leader is a bad one, it can taint a pure soul. A bad leader can do serious harm to a genuinely good soul.

But even then, God is the ultimate leader of souls. And he is stronger than even the worst of leaders in the church, the community, or the world.

 ST. FRANCIS WROTE:

A person may realize that there are many courses of action that would be better and more profitable to his soul than what his superior commands. In such a case, he should make an offering of his own will to God, and do his best to carry out what the superior has asked of him. This is true and loving obedience that is pleasing to God and one's neighbor.

(Admonition 3, part two)

Many who confront this experience of disagreement with a leader often feel they are alone, or are discovering something unique or new. But such a situation is as old as the hills. It is nothing new. Most members of communities or ministries, or even at work, will experience this sooner or later. When we do, we cannot simply leave the community or ministry, or get another job. Maybe in serious and repeated situations where we have taken the appropriate steps to rectify the situations we should leave. But we cannot do so over the normal differences of daily life. By and large, a disagreement cannot be used as an excuse for disobedience.

St. Francis's solution is a fairly standard treatment of monastic obedience. Language like this exists in the Rule of St. Benedict as well. The Rule says that we should see Christ in the abbot or abbess. If at times we do not agree with what we are being asked to do, or even feel that we are unable to carry out a command, we should humbly make our disagreement known to the leader. But if the abbot or abbess still wants us to do what they have asked, we are to make an offering of our self to God, and carry it out as best we can. Plus, we are to do this without any interior grumbling or complaining. Such interior negativity would make it an act of disobedience before God. This is radical stuff, and completely countercultural to the ordinary way of operating in the modern individualistic and secularist West.

This Admonition had special significance for the early Franciscan movement. The friars were often accused of being what the Rule called *sarabaites* or *gyrovagues*, those who wandered from place to place without being under obedience to a superior. Of sarabaites it says, "Two or three together, or even alone, without a shepherd, they pen themselves up in their own sheepfolds, not the Lord's. Their law is what they like to do, whatever strikes their fancy. Anything they believe in and choose, they call holy; anything they dislike, they consider forbidden." And of gyrovagues it continues, "Fourth and finally, there are the monks called gyrovagues, who spend their entire lives drifting from region to region, staying as guests for three or four days in different monasteries. Always on the move, they never settle down, and are slaves to their own wills and gross appetites."

Isolated individuals, or small groups of hermits and itinerants, faced the same accusation years earlier. The likes of St. Romuald addressed this by organizing hermits under obedience to an abbot from their own group, or from an existing monastery. In the time of the Desert Fathers and Mothers they wanted all new monks to be trained under a spiritual father or mother, or an elder brother or sister, to be taught how to avoid the common and treacherous pitfalls of solitary life in the desert. Those who failed to submit to such leadership often came to a terrible end. St. Francis did the same for itinerant hermits and preachers.

In Francis's day, there were many new groups of itinerant hermits and preachers who got themselves into real trouble by not being under a superior. Sometimes this was as simple as degenerating into a disordered lifestyle that was not conducive to good contemplation. Sometimes it was much more serious. These latter cases often involved growing independence from legitimate church leadership, and then lapsing into some errant theology or questionable moral practices. Some of these were major, and tragic.

The purpose in submission was not to force someone into a life of slavish servitude, but to allow him or her to freely choose a life of service. There is a difference. One seeks to enslave well-meaning people under the dictatorship of another, albeit in the name of God. The other seeks to train folks to freely follow Jesus better under the ultimate inspiration of the Holy Spirit. The second is our purpose in religious obedience.

This also has special significance for us today. There are many "lone ranger Christians" out there. There are also many in the so-called New Age movement who want all the benefits of the great spiritual masters of the major religious traditions of the world, but without actually submitting themselves to the discipline and guidance of those same masters. Despite the best of intentions, these lone ranger Christians can often do real spiritual, mental, and emotional harm to themselves and to others if they do not place themselves under good and appropriate spiritual direction and leadership.

At the other end of the spectrum are those who have submitted to leaders who have done harm to their followers and members of their communities. Just as good liturgy builds faith and bad liturgy destroys faith, so good leadership builds

faith and bad leadership destroys faith. Those who have
been hurt and torn down often need healing and restoration
through good and balanced leadership.

Ironically, this also applies to the new ultra-conservatives of
the church. They are often stridently vocal about the seeming
heterodoxy of clergy and religious, or of anything after Vatican
II. But when it really comes down to obedience, they opt
for an essentially Protestant reaction. They refuse to comply
with even the most moderate challenge to their position if it
requires change.

Pope Francis has warned us of the "neo-Pelagians" in our
midst, or those who rely overly on perfection in external
rubrics regarding liturgy and unbendingly rigid morality,
as a way to somehow work their way to heaven. As he and
others have pointed out, this flies in the face of good Catholic
teaching, which is clear that salvation is a gift, or grace, from
God, and while orthodox teaching is important, there is room
for pastoral discretion in applying the law of Christ to those in
most need of his mercy. But when confronted with this, some
choose to hang on to the law rather than grace, and they miss
Christ while claiming to serve him.

Do we seek out those who have more experience than we
do in spiritual life to help us on our way? Are we willing to
really listen to what they have to say, even when we do not
always understand or initially agree? Entering into a good
relationship with a good spiritual leader is one of the greatest
personal gifts that God gave to me in my formative years. Even
now I still need the input of another to help me sort things out
from time to time. I would not trade this for all the so-called
freedom the world can offer.

ST. FRANCIS WROTE:

If a superior commands anything that is against your conscience, you should not spurn his authority, even though you cannot obey. If anyone persecutes you because of this, you should love your superior all the more, for God's sake. A religious who prefers to suffer persecution rather than be separated from his confreres certainly perseveres in true obedience, because he lays down his life for his brethren. There are many religious who under the pretext of doing something more perfect than what their superior commands look behind and go back to their own will that they have given up. People like that are murderers, and by their bad example they cause the loss of many souls.

(Admonition 3, part three)

This sounds radical to modern ears! But this is where St. Francis ushers us into a more developed concept of obedience that wasn't really present in the monastic tradition before him. It is a far cry from the individualistic do-your-own-thing mentality of the modern West. Part three of Admonition 3 is most challenging!

Obedience is not absolute. Yes, there are ancient monastic stories about learning to plant cabbages upside down, or planting a dead limb in the desert, and seeing them bloom and blossom when the deed is done out of humble obedience. These emphasize the need for serious obedience to a good spiritual father or mother, or elder brother or sister. But many a bad leader has abused a member through wrong obedience. This is always tragic. Both the church and good monastic and Franciscan traditions offer real checks and balances to help avoid this problem whenever possible.

Francis recognizes that there are times when a member cannot follow a particular direction of his or her leader. But this does not mean that they become disobedient in other directions from the same leader. This has all kinds of ramifications for us today.

In this Admonition, the guiding light is one's conscience. The problem is that a good conscience isn't automatic. It is a birthright, but it is not given automatically at birth. A good conscience must be formed. This begins in our infancy and youth and continues throughout our life. How is it properly formed? This is done through the teachings of the church regarding matters of faith and morality. It is also done for those in communities through proper community teachings from the Spirit-filled leaders guided by the rule and constitutions of the community within the church.

Many times, we claim "conscience" in cases that are really a matter of personal likes or dislikes. But, as we have seen earlier, regarding the tripartite explanation of the human person, such things are usually the result of the displaced ego. Conscience usually treats major issues. It cannot be used as an excuse for ego or pride, even when parading in the name of spirituality or religion.

Francis says that even if you cannot always obey in one matter, you are not to "spurn the authority" of the leader. In other words, you are not to assume that because you think they got it wrong once, they will always get it wrong. All leaders make mistakes. A community that is intolerant of such mistakes will never find a leader satisfactory and will eventually cease to be a community. It will become a gathering of spiritual anarchists.

Francis says that we are to remain obedient, even when others persecute us for doing so. Sometimes the ones doing the persecuting are trying to get us to be disobedient to a leader they do not like either. Sometimes it is actually the leader who persecutes us through lack of understanding, or through their anger that expresses itself in a mean-spirited way. Either way, remaining obedient in such times takes great humility and maturity.

The fact is that most often when we have problems with leadership, the contentious issue rests on a difference of personal opinion, likes and dislikes, or it's an issue of our not getting our way in some small matter. Such things can get under our skin! Rarely does the trouble have to do with the "big stuff" regarding the teaching of the church, regarding faith and morality, or the community's rule and constitutions. In these things, when the matter is really and truly "small," we are asked to make a sacrifice of our own will and simply do what the leader asks us to do. No great harm comes from it. Life goes on.

Here at the Hermitage we say that whether one perseveres is rarely a matter of the big things of faith, morality, or of community vision or teaching. We say that one must learn to grow a "green bean for God." We may think that we can grow it better than the way we have been asked to do it. When the time is right we can humbly express that thought to our work leader without pride. But they might still ask us to do it their way. At that point we must learn how to simply do what has been asked of us, and to do it cheerfully for God. No major harm will come from it. The garden will still grow, and the farm will still produce. We just might not get it done our way. Some people can live with that. Others can't. Those who can't usually leave. Unfortunately, they often experience the same pattern in the secular workplace or in other religious communities.

We are to obey our duly elected or appointed spiritual leaders as long as they are leading according to the teaching of the church in matters of faith and morality, and the rule, constitutions, and statutes of our community or ministry. They may make some mistakes in these areas. Even in other less major areas some bad decisions might have harmful effects if they become habitual. But unless these do become habitual, or scandalous or seriously harmful, we need not take action.

Plus, we obey with joy! Hebrews says, "Obey your leaders and submit to them; for they are keeping watch over your souls, as men who will have to give account. Let them do this joyfully, and not sadly, for that would be of no advantage to you" (Heb. 13:17). In other words, when we resist our leaders it makes their job drudgery. When that happens, they become less effective, and it hurts the community, every member of it.

In serious cases, there is a proper process we go through based on Scripture. We are first to talk to the leader personally, and to humbly make our opinions known. If that doesn't work then we bring in one or two others directly involved. If that doesn't work then we take it to the community in general through a leadership council or community chapter of professed members. Only as a last resort do we take it to the local bishop, or the pope. On all levels mutual pastoral care, not punishment and anger, are to rule our relations with one another.

As I wrote at the outset, this is all a very ancient problem. At times it challenges us all. The Rule of St. Benedict admits that brothers can elect bad abbots and provides a glimpse at what to do if this happens. The early Franciscans even once appealed to the pope himself to have Brother Elias deposed from leadership. And it worked! (But that episode remains a sad tragedy in the early history of the Franciscan order.)

Francis concludes the Admonition with a warning. He says that under the pretext of doing something better, many disobey their spiritual leaders and follow their own will. The fact of the matter is that this is what most disobedience is really all about. It is rarely about big issues. Francis actually calls these folks "murderers"! This is because such actions eventually will break down the spirit of an entire community. If we all do our own will whenever we do not like what our spiritual leaders ask of us, then we are not a community anymore. We are simply a loose-knit group of individuals who "kind of" believe and live the same way. We end up with spiritual anarchy. This is certainly not what Francis had in mind.

How do we do with this kind of obedience? Do we obey only when we agree with our spiritual leaders, or have we learned to find the will of God in them when they direct according to the gospel, the church, and our community or ministry? Have we learned to appropriately silence our noisy ego and pride in order to really hear the voice of God? If we learn these things, then we will come to perfect obedience, and we will come to perfect peace.

Admonition 4
No One Should Claim the Office of Superior as His Own

〰️ ST. FRANCIS WROTE:

Our Lord tells us, "The Son of Man came not to be served but to serve" (Matt. 20:28). Those who are put in charge of others should be no more proud of their office than if they had been appointed to wash the feet of their confreres.

(Admonition 4, part one)

A s I've mentioned, I'm a founder of a monastic community. I've had to deeply ponder this Admonition many times. Who am I to found a community? Shouldn't I have just joined an existing community in the church? God knows there are plenty of them! Actually, that was my original idea. It was only after discernment with my spiritual father that he encouraged me to found the Brothers and Sisters of Charity. He said that the vision God gave me simply wouldn't fit into existing categories. It was like new wine that would burst the wineskins of the older community structures. So I sought guidance in how to do that from older communities, and they assisted me in finding a home in the church according to canon law. I love the older communities like a mother, but our community is a child of the family that is unique and new.

Such a situation was familiar to St. Francis himself, who was called by God to found a community of his own rather than join an existing monastic community. He tried the Benedictines briefly, and settled for the Order of Penance. (They were not, of course, called Franciscans, at first!) It was only when things unfolded naturally that he founded a new community with the assistance of the bishop of Assisi, Cardinal Hugolino, and Pope Innocent III.

This is one of the short and sweet Admonitions. It seems self-explanatory, but there are some insights that can be added. The first is to note that Francis views the role of leadership as a role of service alone. It has nothing to do with personal honors.

In the time of Francis, the role of the local monastic abbot or prior had often degenerated into a role of great personal power and prestige. This was inherited from the feudal system. In the feudal system, each local area had a "lord," or the one who turned the wheat into bread. These lords received tithes from the churches in their territory, and taxes from the farms and villages.

A prince or duke often endowed monasteries with feudal land and estates to supply them with a means of support. The abbot or prior was established as the local feudal lord. So he became "landed gentry." As long as those in power remained real servants, this system worked pretty well. But by the time of Francis many of the abbots and priors did not resist the temptation to abuse the power, or at least not to reform it, so they represented great wealth instead of gospel poverty and humility.

Francis uses new language to reestablish the role of service for all leaders in his new community. He goes so far as to call the local minister a *custos,* or "custodian," in another place. This means that for Francis the role of the leader was basically that of the janitor!

Anyone who has been in spiritual leadership knows how true this is. If one seeks leadership because they want honors, they are in for a real shock! Spiritual leadership is a crucible in which one is tested. If one is somewhat holy it can either make you more so, or it can take away the little holiness you think you have. It can make you "lose your salvation," or it can help you to be saved.

Leadership essentially strips a person of their egocentric self. We may fight this with an assertion of self through egoism, but eventually even that will fail under the burden of leadership. If we fight it we become miserable, and make everyone around us miserable as well. If we let go of ego, and let the stripping unfold, then we are at peace, and we spread that peacefulness to others through our leadership. The only way to bear such a burden is to release this ego-stripping experience in leadership through the complete relinquishing of self through the cross of Christ.

A modern experience of leadership is sometimes a little less easy. Modern anti-authority attitudes mean that leaders are often accused of all sorts of things. Some may be true. Many are not. In all cases, we seriously consider what is said, do a personal inventory, and repent when we are in the wrong. Today, leaders bear the full brunt of individuals' problems with church, society, and community. One special area is problems with parent figures, or the proverbial "mommy" and "daddy" issues. If these are not resolved before one enters a community or monastery, success under even a great leader is unlikely. And most are not great, they are just adequate, or good, much like all the rest of us!

Dan O'Neill, the founder and first leader in the Christian relief and development organization called Mercy Corps, once described leadership as the "nosecone of a rocket." Whatever the rocket collides with, the nosecone bears the full weight of the impact. This is an apt description. It may or may not be the leader's fault that the collision occurs, but they will bear the heaviest impact out of all the membership of a community. It just goes with the job.

I don't mean to paint an overly negative picture of leadership—but it's important to be honest and dispel any illusions one might have of gaining honors and glory from leadership. It simply doesn't happen—at least not today. Francis was well ahead of the curve by calling the leaders of the community "footwashers" and "custodians." And, of course, Francis inherited such understanding of true spiritual leadership from his master, Jesus.

Footwashing isn't a pretty job. Feet are often stinky, dirty, calloused, and craggy things. This is both metaphor and reality. To wash feet means being willing to get your hands dirty and to touch the "untouchable" things of another person's life. Scripture tells us that feet get dirty by simply walking through the normal things of daily life. These are usually the little failings of life with others. Sometimes it involves big issues. The footwasher helps regular people wash off the dirt accumulated through the daily ups and downs of life. This is rarely romantic or fun, and it usually involves much hard work and little recognition.

But there is also something very precious about being a footwasher. Indeed, it is a very tender image. A good leader must be tender and kind when they remove the dust and grime of daily life from their brothers' and sisters' feet. Here at the Hermitage, we often celebrate a Christian Passover supper on Holy Thursday with a footwashing service. The three Synoptic Gospels imply that the Eucharist was instituted within the context of the Passover. Part of that supper is the washing of hands. Many scholars believe that this is where Jesus instituted washing the disciples' feet.

The leaders begin by washing the feet of those next to them. Then the basin and towel is passed from person to person. As they make their way around the low tables, people are deeply touched. Often, we are moved to loving tears. The tender act of embracing someone else's feet in one's hands, pouring warm water over them, and drying them with a towel brings out the humanity of both the one whose feet are being washed and the one who is washing the other's feet. If you do it right you will never approach that person in the same way again. It must always be done with love and tenderness.

There is a time to scrub the dirt off with "elbow grease." I am reminded of the image of my mother doing a quick scrubbing of my face before church or a doctor's appointment. But she was careful not to damage the skin in scrubbing too hard or too often. Generally, a more tender washing does far better.

Francis says that leaders are to be footwashers. Jesus used this analogy first as an example of service for the apostles, who would be the leaders of the new community that gathered around the teaching and life of Jesus.

Do we think that if we can get into leadership, we will finally have our way? Think again! Usually leaders work twice as hard and bear ten times the stress of the rank-and-file member or worker in a community, ministry, or secular job. If we are in leadership, do we use the power we have with great tenderness and care, or do we scrub too hard to get the job done? The gentle way usually works better. Only occasionally do we ever have to be tough, and even then there is usually a price to pay in the long run.

ST. FRANCIS WROTE:

They should be no more upset at the loss of their authority than they would be if they were deprived of the task of washing feet. The more they are upset, the greater the risk they incur to their souls.

(Admonition 4, part two)

These are sobering words! This part of the Admonition is written for those in leadership, but it applies to everyone. It might be helpful to understand the world of religious leadership in the time of St. Francis before we apply it to every situation.

In the early days of the Franciscan movement Francis was the unquestioned leader. He was the spiritual father and "mother" of the community. Earthly moms and dads are for life. It was assumed that he would remain in leadership for life, but serious health issues, and his own humility, caused him to resign a few years before his death in 1226. Even his successors were originally envisioned as being for a life term. It was only after a really bad leader in Brother Elias that this changed, and after that, general ministers were elected for a specific term. They could lose their position of leadership.

Other leaders could also come and go. Leadership was needed on every level of the community. There were local, regional, and international leaders. Some were primary on their level, and some were in roles assisting the primary leaders. Specifically, they had "ministers" and "vicar ministers." Other roles and titles also developed.

Monasticism went through a similar evolution. Originally, abbots and abbesses were in a lifetime position of spiritual leadership. They could be removed under extraordinary circumstances. Some later monastic communities chose an elected term for their abbots and abbesses. Some retained a life term with the possibility of retirement. Most found that after twelve or so years most abbots and abbesses had given all they could to their communities and were ready to retire. All of them had priors, prioresses, and other roles of leadership to assist the abbot or abbess of the monastic community to function on a day in, day out practical level. These were not permanent positions.

This all predated Francis, with the eleventh-century reforms of Romuald and Bruno and the Camaldolese and Carthusians, respectively. The newer communities often did away with the title of abbot altogether, and opted to simply call their leaders "priors," with limited terms. This avoided the issue altogether. The Carthusians originally had the prior submit his resignation at every general chapter, only to continue if the chapter confirmed him for another year. There is some wisdom here. But I tend to like the life term, with the leader growing in wisdom as they mature.

My own experience as spiritual father of our community has revealed a pattern. In the beginning, I was usually unsure of myself, timid, and perhaps too weak. Then I corrected this by asserting my role, but I was sometimes too strong. After many years, I found more of a balance between the two extremes. As a founder who started quite young, I am grateful that I had a lengthier time to learn how to get it right, and I'm equally grateful for the patience of the community as I did. Even now, I still make my share of mistakes! The problem is that by the time many of us get to the point where we finally "get it," we are so tired that we are ready to retire! Maybe that's not such a bad thing either.

At one particularly painful time in our community's development, I actually submitted my resignation to our bishop. This required a complete relinquishment of my ego attachment. But it somehow felt very good. He told me I was taking the easy way out and refused to accept it. Later, after a member resisted me with an anger that was verbally violent in a general community meeting, I had been hungering for solitude anyway, so I again submitted my resignation to the community. Again, they wouldn't accept it. Only with great hesitance did I comply. I suspect there is a time coming when I will retire from leadership in favor of greater solitude. But it will require a change of a position I have held for decades and will therefore demand a total rethinking of what I do with my time. It will no doubt be an adjustment, to say the least.

Francis wanted those in leadership to be ready to step down the minute they were asked to do so. He wanted them to do this joyfully, and without losing their inner peace. For most of us who have endured long years of the ups and downs of leadership, and if there is a qualified person to take our place, this is quite a blessing. It is something we welcome.

But it does not always work this way. We often get quite attached to our role of service as a point of personal identity. This identity is false. Our real identity lies not in what we do, but in who we are before God. While we are all called to different positions of service in this life, and God wants us to do a good job, we do not stand before God as leaders or workers. We stand before God as a naked soul, a child of God just like everyone else. St. John of the Cross once said that all God will ask after we die is how well we have loved. That sounds so simple, but it is an all-inclusive and comprehensive question! All Christian theology, ecclesiology, sacraments, mysticism, and lifestyle are wrapped up in our answer.

I must admit a similar pattern regarding my music ministry. For decades, I have tried to stay focused on my *being* rather than on my *ministry*. I have taught, and truly believed, that this is the only way that a ministry can be truly free to accomplish God's will. But as I have grown older, and more of my followers have grown older and even died, I find an entire generation that doesn't know who I am. This is disconcerting for someone who filled churches and concert halls for decades! Suddenly I am growing forgotten and irrelevant by the next generation.

This is the common pattern for any retiree. We all come to a time in our life when we must retire from active service, and let the next generation have their turn at the wheel. In most cultures of the past it is at this point that we take a venerable position of elder. In ancient cultures older was better, and newer was only cautiously accepted. Unfortunately, in our culture, new is always better, and old is almost completely irrelevant. So when we retire today, we must really embrace a letting go of old attachments to leadership and function that is perhaps new to our novelty-driven culture. But we must do it nonetheless. As St. Francis said, "I have done my part, may Christ teach you yours." And, "Brothers, let us now begin, for up until now we have done nothing."

How do we become so attached to what we are as an identity of who we are? I believe that it is because we get the biblical priorities of spirit, soul, and body fouled up and turned upside down. We mistakenly identify too much with our sensual, emotional, and mental faculties and energies as our most essential self. When we do not get the sensual pleasure, the recognition, or the control we want, we become emotionally upset. This confuses our mind. When we cannot focus on God's will with our mind, then we focus on our own. Then we get upset again. This causes physical stress and illness. The spirit, the deepest and most essential part of who we are, gets almost completely forgotten. And so it goes.

When we allow our identity to become confused and focus on the more external faculties of our being, then we find it difficult to let go of the more external aspects of our life when the time comes. We attach our personal identity to our function, rather than letting our function flow from our personal identity in Christ. When we do that our ministries are free to be what God wants them to be, rather than what we limit them to.

The way out of all this is through the cross of Jesus. The practical aids in this letting go of my old, or false self, are found in prayerful liturgy, sacraments, devotions, private meditation, and healthy ascetical disciplines, not to mention life in the church and monastic community and family. They are the mechanics and methods employed. But they are only the road maps and aids, not the destination and goal. When we let go of this false self, then we find out who we really are in God, and do not get so upset when the external things like job descriptions and such come and go. When we do this, we discover the truth of what St. Francis is describing in this Admonition.

I've also noticed that many people drop out of active participation, or even leave a community, once their leadership term is expired. I've always found this disappointing. It always makes me sad. I understand that our American understanding of retirement lends itself to such actions. But, while we can retire from a role in community, we can never retire from a community that we are really members of. Only those who are never really members of a community can leave it (1 John 2:19). I am so impressed when those who move out of leadership remain humble servants of the community and our ministries once they join the regular membership again. It stirs me to greater admiration of them as people, followers of Jesus, and to greater faith in Christ.

Each must ask himself or herself, have we attached our egos to our position, or to our work? A great test is to ask ourselves: If I lose the ability or opportunity to continue in that position, do I become upset and angry? If so, we have become attached.

This attachment and loss steals our inner peace and separates us from the full experience of the grace and peace of Jesus Christ. Only by letting go of our role daily can we fulfill it consistently. But this is a tall order. It is simple, but rarely easy. It requires a real change of old ego patterns that identify our self-worth with the job we do rather than in the person we are in Jesus Christ. When we do not really know who we are in Jesus, then we attach our identity to our job, and we are easily upset and angry when we lose control of these things. When we are confident of who we are in Jesus, then we are free to do anything we are asked to do, whether big or small, whether things we will be noticed for and things that only Jesus sees.

If we really let go of the false self, we will be ready for whatever comes. We will be ready to accept any role of service. We will also be ready to let go of one. But God will always show us another role of service wherever we are, and in whatever we do. We need not feel bad if we are removed from a position of leadership, or from a job we really like. Remember the old saying, "Whenever God closes a door, he opens a window!" Let's open the windows of our life to the Spirit of God. Then we will understand this Admonition, and then we will be happy anywhere we are.

Admonition 5
Don't Give Way to Pride

ST. FRANCIS WROTE:

Try to realize the dignity God has conferred on you. He created and formed your body in the image of his beloved Son, and your soul in his likeness. Yet every creature under heaven serves, acknowledges, and obeys its Creator in its own way better than you do. Even the devils were not solely responsible for crucifying him; you who crucified him with them, and you continue to crucify him by taking pleasure in your vices and sins. What are you proud about? If you were so clever and learned that you knew everything and could speak every language, so that the things of heaven were an open book to you, still you could not boast. Any of the devils knew more about the things of heaven, and know more about the things of earth, than any human being, even one who might have received from God a special revelation of the highest wisdom. If you were the most handsome and the richest in the world, and could work wonders and drive out devils, all that would be something extrinsic to you; it would not belong to you and you could not boast of it. There is only one thing of which we can boast: our humiliations, and taking up daily the holy cross of our Lord Jesus Christ (see 1 Cor. 13; 2 Cor. 12:5).

In the previous chapter I shared some of the things I am letting go of. Now I am wondering, what is really ours in the first place? This is the inescapable question that comes to mind with this Admonition.

I mentioned letting go of leadership, or even of my active ministry. This is hard. But are they really mine? No, they aren't. They are gifts from God, so God can take them back, or give them to someone else anytime he sees fit to do so. We all have our own version of such relinquishment of control over our life or work. But it really goes much deeper than this.

God creates us. All that we are is a gift from God. In this sense, nothing that we have belongs to us alone. It belongs to God. We are only stewards of those gifts.

God creates us in his image. This makes the human being unique. But no one has successfully defined what this really means. We used to think that it was the ability to reason, or to use language, or to love that made humans unique. But tests have shown that various animals also share these faculties. Some have said that it is our Trinitarian makeup that establishes us uniquely in the image of God. Scripture describes us as "spirit, soul, and body." Scholasticism used the description of "memory, intellect, and will." This is interesting, though not always convincing. All the various attempts to define our uniqueness in terms of rational thought, or language, or even love have eventually all failed as we find these attributes in animals as well.

Yet the uniqueness of the human being is self-evident. If nothing else displays it, it is our unique ability among the animal world to affect the entire environment with our technology for the better or the worse. Though some other creatures like dolphins even appear to be smarter than we are, no other creature has such radical effects on creation as does the human being. But descriptions remain mere human attempts to explain this truth that is at once both mysterious and self-evident.

What is certain is that this gift is the most complete gift that God can give to a creature. It is a profoundly distinct honor to carry within us the image and likeness of God. St. Bonaventure would say that while the human being bears God's image, the rest of creation bears his "traces." This truth inspires us to care for and reverence the rest of creation with the same reverence that we give to the sacred things of God. But we alone carry his image.

Francis emphasizes that we often have not carried this divine gift well. He juxtaposes us with the devils, who are considered the most wicked of all creation because of their unrepentant rejection of God. Yet he says that even they did not crucify Jesus. That is something that we did on our own. We cannot say "the devil made me do it." We must take that terrible responsibility on ourselves.

We might say, "When did I crucify Jesus?" Jesus says that we deny him every time we deny his love to "the least of these," his "little ones" (Matt. 25:45). Francis says that we do this every time we knowingly sin. Hebrews 6:4–6 says the same thing: "if they then commit apostasy, since they crucify the Son of God on their own account and hold him up to contempt." This is especially true regarding sins that we know to be of major moral consequence through revelation, and empowerment to fulfill them has been given us by the Holy Spirit. But it applies to a life of habitual "little sins" as well.

Nor can we boast in any of the good things in our lives. These are gifts from God that flow back to his glory. Plus, most of these things are "extrinsic" to our essential being. They are external to the internal and real us. Good looks, intelligence or talent, or any other such thing is still not part of who we essentially are. They are extrinsic to our spirit, to our essence. They are only external gifts given to us by God. Plus, even the devils are smarter and more talented than we are, and look where it got them! Real spiritual merit lies elsewhere. Spirit and soul are the deeper realities in our life. The physical faculties of bodily senses and the physical aspects of thought and emotion are certainly part of us. We are created spirit, soul, and body, and we believe in the resurrection of the body, though it will be transformed into something far more wonderful than what we currently experience. But they are just the vehicles for this deeper dimension of the human being, the soul and the spirit.

We need only think of those whom we know who are diagnosed with diseases such as Parkinson's or Alzheimer's. Or just think of getting old. As they say, "Getting old ain't for sissies!" Regardless of our intellectual skills or physical attributes, skills, and talents, we lose most of these things before we die, and we discover in the final days of our life the essential person that lay beneath those external things.

This includes human knowledge. As St. Paul said, "Love never ends; . . . as for knowledge, it will pass away" (1 Cor. 13:8). The Jews respected those who knew the Law, the Prophets, and the Mishnah almost by heart. The Greeks respected those knowledgeable in philosophical wisdom. Today, we often confuse *knowledge about* God with actually *knowing* God. This is just pseudo-theology. Real theology is rooted in the mystical knowing of God.

St. Paul said,

> Where is the wise man? Where is the scribe? Where is the debater of this age? Has not God made foolish the wisdom of the world? For since, in the wisdom of God, the world did not know God through wisdom, it pleased God through the folly of what we preach to save those who believe. For Jews demand signs and Greeks seek wisdom, but we preach Christ crucified, a stumbling block to Jews and folly to Gentiles, but to those who are called, both Jews and Greeks, Christ the power of God and the wisdom of God. (1 Cor. 1:20–24)

Further on, Paul elaborates true wisdom as it relates to the cross of Jesus Christ and the power of the Spirit:

> When I came to you, brethren, I did not come proclaiming to you the testimony of God in lofty words or wisdom. For I decided to know nothing among you except Jesus Christ and him crucified. And I was with you in weakness and in much fear and trembling; and my speech and my message were not in plausible words of wisdom, but in demonstration of the Spirit and power, that your faith might not rest in the wisdom of men but in the power of God.
>
> Yet among the mature we do impart wisdom, although it is not a wisdom of this age or of the rulers of this age, who are doomed to pass away. But we impart a secret and hidden wisdom of God, which God decreed before the ages for our glorification. None of the rulers of this age understood this; for if they had, they would not have crucified the Lord of glory. But, as it is written,
> "What no eye has seen, nor ear heard,
> nor the heart of man conceived,
> what God has prepared for those who love him,
> God has revealed to us through the Spirit."
> (1 Cor. 2:1–10)

Accordingly, St. Francis is often said to have taken a dim view of theology. But this is a one-sided view that is at best incomplete. Francis was critical of pseudo-theology, not the real deal. Most of all, Francis objected to the pride that often comes from theological knowledge. In this he agreed with St. Paul, who said, "'Knowledge' puffs up, but love builds up" (1 Cor. 8:1).

Some theologians think that they alone really know the truth about God, and regular Christians are left on the outside looking in. In my experience, none of the great theologians hold this view. The real giants of theology I have had the privilege to meet (and they are rare) are most aware that the more they have learned about God, the more they realize how little they actually know. So, for the real theologian their theological knowledge humbles them; it does not give way to pride. It is only the "would-be" theologians who carry that pride from an external knowledge that generates arrogance and pride.

St. Francis is cautious of the brothers learning theology because it so easily leads to pride. He, for instance, once wrote to St. Anthony of Padua and commissioned him to teach theology to the friars who might benefit from it, but on the one condition that their prayer life, their devotion, should remain primary, and not be hindered by excessive emphasis on books. But he didn't look down on theologians either. He instructed the brothers to show real respect for all bishops, priests, deacons, religious, and theologians. Francis's caution regarding the pride that accompanies theological study, or even ordination, cannot be construed as a rejection of either.

Following the teaching of Evagrius, that "a real theologian is one who prays, and one who prays is a real theologian," the Eastern Christian tradition tends to emphasize that one is only given a degree in theology when one has first discovered a mystical encounter with God through Jesus Christ in the Holy Spirit. This is because real theology isn't something external to us, but something that is given by the Holy Spirit into our deepest heart and soul. It is spiritual, and it enlivens the mind. But it remains a gift of God, not something we take human pride in.

The monastic fathers say that there are three powers: divine, human, and demonic. God and his angels and the devil can inspire or tempt us respectively by placing thoughts into our mind. But it is up to us what we do with those things. We must ultimately cooperate with grace for our relationship with

Jesus to be one of real love. God can empower us to respond through his Spirit within us, but we must do our part as well. And the Spirit gives even that cooperation with grace to us. All power essentially comes from God. Humans and demons are creatures of God. The demons rebelled and tried to use their gifts apart from God. But that doesn't work. They can only pervert what God has already given. This leads to frustration, anger, bitterness, and death. It leads to hell. The demons try to get us to join them in their rebellion. We have the power to choose and resist, but only when we open ourselves to the power of God through grace.

St. Francis says in this Admonition that the only thing that is ours is what we choose to do with those gifts. We own this completely. But we cannot even *want* to make the right choice without his gift of the Spirit of grace that orients us to want to do this in the first place. Furthermore, we cannot carry out that choice without his help. St. Paul's Letter to the Philippians says, "for God is at work in you, both to will and to work for his good pleasure" (Phil. 2:13). Psalm 16:2 says, "I say to the LORD, 'Thou art my Lord; I have no good apart from thee.'" The only thing that we can really do on our own is to reject this great gift. And this is a lie. We are his creation, and we cannot exist independent of God. All else is illusion. To live a life based on illusion is delusion.

The greatest thing that we can choose is the cross of Jesus. This is the highest truth of the Christian faith. It is the Paradox of paradoxes. Every major religion teaches that, after some basic objective truths regarding faith and morality, the greater mystical truths are only reached through paradox. A paradox is an apparent contradiction that carries a deeper truth. These would include finding God's deepest word in silence, or most intense companionship in solitude, or wealth in poverty, and the like. Jesus not only teaches these paradoxes. He *is* this paradox. Other great religions may point to the way, the truth, and the life, and even do so quite beautifully, but only Jesus is the way, truth, and life fully incarnated beyond an idea into a perfect life that is fully God and fully man.

The greatest thing we can do as followers of Jesus is to take up our own cross to find this way of paradox. In one of my songs I quote St. Paul, who says, "May I never boast of anything, save the cross of the Lord. The cross of Jesus Christ." This is the clear teaching of St. Francis of Assisi as well.

Admonition 6
The Imitation of Christ

ST. FRANCIS WROTE:

Look at the Good Shepherd, my brothers. To save his sheep he endured the agony of the cross. They followed him in trials and persecutions, in disgrace and dishonor, hunger and thirst, in humiliations and temptations, and so on. And for this God rewarded them with eternal life. We ought to be ashamed of ourselves; the saints endured all that, but we who are servants of God try to win honor and glory by recounting and making known what we have done.

Catholics love to tell the stories of the saints. Saints Francis and Clare, Saints Benedict and Scholastica, St. Antony and St. Pachomius of the Desert are all monastic saints close to my heart. They are the patron saints of my integrated monastic community. We love to talk about Mary, the Theotokos, the *bearer*, or the Mother of God. This book is about St. Francis. I believe that it is good to tell these stories. But we must be careful.

It is so easy to spend years studying the lives and teachings of the saints, and to somehow think that we have become saintly. But it is not enough just to read—we must also live. G. K. Chesterton once said that St. Francis is too easily a lovely saint who warms our heart with his simplicity and quaint teachings, while we read about him in an easy chair before a cozy fireplace, or outside in the beauty of nature. He is only appealing to most of us when he's seated *downwind!* In other words, Francis was a scrappy little guy who probably smelled bad, and looked ill kept, scantily clad, and desperately poor. He was certainly not socially acceptable when he first appeared on the scene!

I remember my own vocation and the beginning of our religious community. We were birthed from the Franciscan tradition. But sometimes I have been too much about St. Francis. The same thing can happen with my love for monasticism. I read and read a constant flow of books about monks and monastic history, great and small. I truly love it. But sometimes I find myself creating an idol of Franciscanism and monasticism. I forget that it is all ultimately about Jesus.

About the time I was really beginning to settle deeply into Franciscanism, I received an inner word that said, "Die to Franciscanism!" What? I loved St. Francis and Franciscanism. How could I "die" to it? Then it dawned on me: I had to learn to be more about Jesus and less about Francis. Likewise, I had to be more about Francis and less about Franciscanism. So in the community we learned to say that Franciscanism is our mother, but our community is a child that is unique and new. We love our mother, and we honor our history, but we must be about Jesus first, if we are to really follow the example of St. Francis. This is ultimately true of those who honor or follow any saint.

After all my decades of serious and devoted monastic study, it is still St. Francis that stirs the simplicity of my soul for Jesus when all or everyone else fails. When St. Antony, Sts. Benedict or Scholastica, Sts. Romuald or Bruno or Bernard, or even the simple but profound Desert Fathers or Mothers can't stir me, St. Francis always will! He holds a special place in my heart and soul.

It is true that reading about the saints and things of God is a positive thing. It inspires us. It helps us to meditate, which means to fill the mind with concepts and images. We think in pictures or images. Even conceptual thinking uses images. These images can be good, bad, or neutral. In this case, when we fill our minds and hearts with the saints, we are surrounding ourselves with positive images about God and his servants.

Scripture says that whatever we think deeply about, we become (Prov. 23:7 KJV). Science tells us that when we meditate, the mind slows down and the frequency of our brain waves slows as well. At this point, whatever we think sinks more deeply into our consciousness. The mind slows in this way when we meditate, listen to music, or watch TV and movies. This is why it is so important to fill the mind with good thoughts and images when using the media. As the old saying goes, "Garbage in, garbage out." St. Paul says, "Finally, brethren, whatever is true, whatever is honorable, whatever is just, whatever is pure, whatever is lovely, whatever is gracious, if there is any excellence, if there is anything worthy of praise, *think about these things*" (Phil. 4:8). And, "We have the mind of Christ" (1 Cor. 2:16). This is why it's important to pray and to meditate. The saints will help us.

But it is not enough to simply read and pray. This can come dangerously close to daydreaming. Daydreams are good as long as they actually change the way we live our days. We want to focus the mind on the hope of heaven, but we do not want to be "so heavenly minded that we are no earthly good." Real meditation changes our daily life, and for the better. It clears the mind, directs the emotions, and disciplines the body for better health. It makes us better people.

In the *Philokalia*, St. Nilus the Ascetic agreed with St. Francis when he warned against premature teachers who taught before they had really been taught by life. Specifically, he wanted them to be trained under a good elder before they assumed the role of an elder. He describes the scene with tragic humor. He says that the premature teacher loves to learn the sayings of saints to impress would-be disciples and donors. Soon such a teacher can be found with a bevy of disciples in tow, going from one rich benefactor's house to another, scandalizing the faithful all the while. They end up scandalizing others, losing their donors and disciples, and their own soul in the process. The only cure is to stop quoting and teaching, and to return to humble obedience under an experienced elder.

This can also be the case today, though our culture is different. Today it is done primarily through untested teachers writing books and posting articles and such on social media. I am deeply challenged by this warning! Especially in the West, we sometimes think that just because we have studied spirituality that we are spiritual. Similarly, in the Catholic Church we sometimes think that if there is a problem, send someone to school to get a degree, and that will solve it. There's nothing wrong with folks getting good intellectual training, but that is only part of the solution. The deeper solution is in real spiritual training by an experienced elder. Many of the first Desert Fathers and Mothers were uneducated, simple folk. Just because one has a scholastic degree in spiritual matters does not necessarily mean they are ready to live or teach real spirituality.

This is especially true regarding spiritual direction. There's a saying in the Christian monastic East that it is always better to have a spiritual director than to not have one, but it is better to have no spiritual director than to have a bad one. In the latter case, it is sufficient to read the teachings of the Fathers and their time-tested interpretation of Scripture. Only a fool chooses to have themselves as a spiritual director. So how do we find a good spiritual director?

It is important that a spiritual director be someone who has really lived the life themselves for many years before they presume to direct others. This way of life is best found in the monastic tradition. Though a good thing, it is not enough to simply get a spiritual direction certification. It seems that the older I get, the less confident I am about directing anyone! I am increasingly called to simply be a disciple of Jesus. If anyone wants to follow, that's really up to them.

I sometimes felt like an untested teacher in my early years in ministry. Because of my musical success and monastic way of life I started writing books when I was still young in the ways of God. I had lived as a hermit and placed myself under spiritual direction. I had founded a community and was learning how to make a vision a reality, but I was often far from the wisdom needed to direct others the way that I would like to be directed myself. It is only in the last decades that life has tested me sufficiently to where I feel somewhat ready to share insights with greater confidence and with greater humility. Now it is less about teaching, and more about sharing. And I do that, not as an authority, but as a fellow spiritual traveler on the journey to God.

So, read, yes! Meditate, yes! Get a degree, sure! We can even quote experts from time to time. But it is far more important to live the life of a saint than to read about one.

Admonition 7

Good Works
Must Follow Knowledge

ST. FRANCIS WROTE:

St. Paul tells us, "The letter kills, but the Spirit gives life" (2 Cor. 3:6). A person has been killed by the letter when he wants to know quotations only so that people will think he is learned and he can make money to give to his relatives and friends. A religious person has been killed by the letter when he has no desire to follow the spirit of Sacred Scripture but wants to know what it says so that he can explain it to others. On the other hand, those have received life from the Spirit of Sacred Scripture who, by their words and example, refer to the Most High God, to whom belongs all good, all that they know or wish to know, and do not allow their knowledge to become a source of complacency.

The most obvious theme of this Admonition is a discussion I started in the last chapter. But there are other important themes here as well.

First, St. Francis says that we have to catch the Spirit in Sacred Scripture. Many people quote the Scriptures, but few really get to the Spirit of the Scriptures. St. Bonaventure began his *Breviloquem*, or brief instruction on the church, with the admonition that unless we understand the Holy Spirit who authored Scripture, all our study will be fruitless. St. Thomas Aquinas said pretty much the same thing.

When the Holy Spirit is really indwelling us, and stirred up within and filling us, then Jesus and the Father are within us recognizing their own words in the words of Scripture. Like John the Baptist leaping in his mother's womb at the presence of Jesus in Mary's womb, the Holy Spirit literally leaps up within us when we hear the words of Jesus, or the apostles or the Law and the Prophets. This is because Jesus and the Father are within us recognizing their own words.

The documents of Vatican II teach that Scripture must be interpreted in the same spirit in which it was written. The "Dogmatic Constitution on Divine Revelation," one of those documents, says, "But, since Holy Scripture must be read and interpreted in the sacred spirit in which it was written, no less serious attention must be given to the content and unity of the whole of Scripture if the meaning of the sacred texts is to be correctly worked out. The living tradition of the whole Church must be taken into account along with the harmony which exists between elements of the faith."

This isn't all mystical and charismatic. It takes intellectual understanding as well. This means understanding something of the religious and cultural context, as well as simply learning the literal meanings of the words and ideas. Those words might evoke different images and mean different things today than they did at the time they were written. Sometimes we have to do a little study of these things before we can properly apply the Scriptures to our own situation today. We must read thoughtfully.

It also means being under the inspiration of the Holy Spirit as we read. This means reading prayerfully. Some people think that the Spirit has anointed them when, in reality, they are only excited! To be anointed by the Spirit might include enthusiasm, but its main characteristic is becoming more like Jesus, becoming Christlike. Jesus was a religious Master of masters, a Mystic of mystics, and a Teacher of teachers. He was probably more like a Jewish prophet, or even a Sufi mystic, a Buddhist bodhisattva, than he was like today's megachurch pastor or modern motivational speaker. Sometimes we get the Spirit of Scripture confused with excitement for our interpretation of the Word of God.

Our inspiration from Scripture must also include objective truth. Sacred Scripture is the earliest written expression of the faith of the followers of Jesus Christ. It is apostolic in its authorship, meaning either through the apostles or their direct disciples. It also represents the early church's understanding of the Jewish Scriptures. The widespread use of the written word was something novel in that time. The church used this newest media to spread the word of Jesus Christ. These came in Gospels, which told the story of Jesus, or apostolic letters that applied that gospel to the real situation of local churches, and the church universal.

The Christian Scriptures thus came forth from the authority of the life of the church. It was the bishops who gathered these books with the apostolic authority. You cannot really understand the Scriptures unless you understand the living authority of the early church, which is catholic, universal, and full. We must also understand by living within that living authority and apostolic tradition today.

As the *Catechism of the Catholic Church* explains succinctly: "In order that the full and living Gospel might always be preserved in the Church the apostles left bishops as their successors. They gave them 'their own position of teaching authority.'" Indeed, "the apostolic preaching, which is expressed in a special way in the inspired books, was to be preserved in a continuous line of succession until the end of time." (861) This living transmission is called tradition, not Scripture. "The sayings of the holy Fathers are a witness to the life-giving presence of this Tradition, showing how its riches are poured out in the practice and life of the Church, in her belief and her prayer" (2651).

Does this mean that Scriptures have no authority? Absolutely not! Sacred Scripture is a "canon," or a "measuring stick, or a "plumb line," of all that comes after it. A measuring stick measures all that comes after it, but it does not mean that everything is explicitly contained within it. The universal teachings and principles are there, but not the specifics that arise as the church faces the different questions and challenges that each culture and people encounters as we travel through space and time toward eternity. For something to be "scriptural" means that it is consistent with those universals, but not always explicitly mentioned in the Scriptures.

This balance between apostolic tradition, Sacred Scripture, and the teaching authority of the church is already present in Scripture. St. Paul writes to St. Timothy, "But as for you, continue in what you have learned and have firmly believed, knowing from whom you learned it and how from childhood you have been acquainted with the sacred writings which are able to instruct you for salvation through faith in Christ Jesus. All scripture is inspired by God and profitable for teaching, for reproof, for correction, and for training in righteousness, that the man of God may be complete, equipped for every good work" (2 Tim. 3:14–17). Paul first mentions the living authority of the leaders and community of faith, and then he mentions the Scriptures, meaning the Christian understanding of the Jewish Scriptures. The two go together. You cannot separate them without doing injustice to either.

These objective guidelines must be put into practice if they are to really bear fruit. Learning to integrate study and prayer does this. The monastic tradition has historically been the special school where this art is practiced and perfected. It often describes four stages or steps. Let's examine them briefly and take these time-tested steps.

First, look to the practice of *lectio divina*, or sacred reading. Nowhere in the early sources do we find Francis teaching or clearly practicing the methods of the great spiritual teachers of mystical and contemplative Christianity. But he was, no doubt, at least familiar with them. Plus, Franciscans who followed him used these tools freely in their teachings. St. Bonaventure, for example, was most familiar with the classical methods of contemplative prayer, and he used them freely. He is called the great Franciscan "Seraphic Doctor."

Lectio is only one of four steps in classical monastic approaches to the contemplative life. Lectio involves reading the sacred text slowly and prayerfully. One fills the mind with the entire text using the imagination.

Intimately related to this stage is *oratio*, or "prayer," where we say the words out loud as we pray or form them silently with our lips. Interestingly, this is included in the Jewish understanding on meditating on Scripture. Why? By forming the text with our lips we are forced to slow down. We cannot speed-read the text. Saying the words in this way causes them to sink deeper into the human consciousness. It also aids in memorization.

Third is *meditatio*, or meditation. In this stage, we actively use the imagination to picture the reality described by the words of Scripture. St. Bonaventure says that "imagination assists understanding." Why? We think in pictures. Abstract thought simply does not happen without pictures. Even when doing numbers or words, we usually see them before we understand them. We must "see it" before we can "get it." Meditation uses the human faculty of imagination with the things of God.

This stage stirs up and directs every active human faculty. This includes the thoughts, which direct the emotions, which direct, and are housed by, the bodily senses. So the entire active part of the human being is involved. This also paves the way for the next stage of contemplation.

Remember, we think constantly. We cannot turn the mind off. We even think when we sleep! But we can direct our thoughts and slow them down. We can unclutter our minds of the junk and focus on the real treasure of God and the gospel of Jesus. This leads us to contemplation, where we move beyond thought without ending thought. We move into pure spiritual intuition.

Fourth comes *contemplatio*, or contemplation. In this stage, we build on the senses, emotions, and thoughts but surpass them all with pure spiritual intuition. Contemplation is a pure experience of God that is beyond all thought, names, forms, and ideas. It surpasses emotions and senses. It is pure spiritual experience. While the other faculties involve our created human energies experiencing at least in part God's uncreated energies, contemplation is spirit to Spirit, essence to Essence. Here we simply *are* with the One who Is, the great I AM. This One can be pointed to with ideas and words, but never fully described. This is the goal of all Scripture study, all theology, all sacraments and liturgy; it is really the final end of the church, which exists to bring all people into this full union with God as a united people.

Contemplation is the ultimate ministry. It is the prayer of prayers. Simply by our sitting in contemplation the world is affected on the level of the Spirit in ways that we cannot comprehend. This goes way beyond just "visualizing world peace." This is *being* world peace in the Prince of Peace. Wayne Dyer once told a story of a mystic/quantum physicist who said that it only takes twelve fully enlightened people on the planet at one time to keep the negative energy of the world from causing us to self-destruct. I cannot vouch for the precise accuracy of this calculation, but it certainly jibes with what mystics have said about contemplative prayer for thousands of years. Be peace. Be a contemplative. This will change you, and it change the entire world.

But then don't stop with contemplation alone. Contemplation must change our lives, and for the better! If contemplation is a reservoir, then action is an aqueduct. St. Bernard of Clairvaux said that contemplation is like a resting place to collect the full pressure of the stream before it is channeled back out for others. St. Dominic said that ministers are like aqueducts that channel the water out for others, but do not save any for themselves. We must become reservoirs through contemplation, and then aqueducts of grace through apostolic ministry and action. Many try to be aqueducts without first being a reservoir. But they have little or no water of grace to share, and they end up dried out. In modern ministry, we call this burnout, and it is all too common. Prayer overflows naturally into ministry, and ministry leads both the minister and others naturally back into prayer. One without the other is less than fully Christlike.

St. Francis says that he seeks "not so much to pray, as to become a prayer." Some have used this to justify never praying. This was not Francis's intent. He founded hermitages across Italy specifically for undistracted, contemplative prayer. It was a central component of their way of life.

The contemplative life is the crowning jewel of a fully mature Christian, a local church, a religious community, and the heart of the church. Contemplation is the heartbeat of the church because it is the heartbeat of God. It is contemplation that pumps the lifeblood of Jesus and the power of the Holy Spirit out to others who do ministry. When one prays, we all pray, and when one ministers, we all minister.

Contemplation flows outward into action, and action leads us back into contemplation. Let those who are afraid of contemplation beware of action, and those who are afraid of action beware of contemplation. Neither can be an escape from the other. Both complement the other. This rhythm brings healthy balance to our life in Christ.

Admonition 8
Beware the Sin of Envy

⌇⌇⌇ ST. FRANCIS WROTE:

St. Paul tells us, "No one can say 'Jesus is Lord' except by
the Holy Spirit" (1 Cor. 12:3). And, "None is righteous,
no, not one" (Rom. 3:12). So, if a person envies the good
that God says or does through his brother or sister, it is
like committing a sin of blasphemy, because that person is
really envying God, who is the only source of every good.

St. Francis was big on saying that God is good. He
enthusiastically says that God is all good, every good,
that he alone is good. Francis would probably like the
popular modern chant that goes, "God is good all the time,
and all the time God is good!" The goodness of God became a
chief component in later Franciscan theology as well, in such
greats as St. Bonaventure.

Goodness is described as "self-diffusive." In other words,
goodness must overflow out from itself to and for another. As
St. Paul says of Jesus, it is "self-emptying." This stands in stark
contrast to our present culture of self-obsession and gratification. This is part of the philosophical basis for the plurality
of the Godhead within the one God in Franciscan theology.
Scripture already describes God as one, plural, and neuter in
the Elohist tradition. "Then God said, 'Let us make man in our
image, after our likeness'" (Gen. 1:26).

The reasoning of Bonaventure goes something like this: If God is good, then he must exist for the sake of another. But if God is transcendent and self-sufficient, then he must be completely self-diffusive (or self-giving to another) within his own being. If God must create to satisfy his goodness, then God is no longer transcendent, and can no longer really be God. God is reduced to a mere god. Yet God does create out of goodness, but by an act of his own free will. He didn't have to create in order to fulfill his goodness. So God's goodness is fulfilled within his own one being. This means that he is one, yet many. Love is the union of two to create at least a third. So the goodness and love of God require that God be both one and Trinity. This is perfect logic. It is also perfect paradox.

This kind of goodness only exists perfectly in God. It exists in creation as an extension and gift of God. Any goodness in the human being is something created as a gift, and not something we can claim exclusively as our own. When we try to claim it as our own, then we commit the sin of blasphemy. This is also true of envying God's good gifts given to others. This is the reason St. Francis writes so strongly against envy.

I must confess the sin of envy. I have secretly envied those who enjoyed a success greater than mine or received more recognition. I've thought to myself, and even to God, *Why not me? Didn't I work as hard or have as much talent?* and so on. I know that is petty, but it is part of my fallen condition. And truth be told, not only did God keep me from greater fame to save me from a runaway ego, but also others were simply more talented or gifted than I was. And they worked harder than I did! My envy is usually without justification. It all comes from my ego and pride.

Envy is one of the seven cardinal sins as listed in the Christian West. In the Christian East, it is not directly listed, but is assumed as part of the list of what's called the eight thoughts. It really comes from two: self-glory and boredom, or acedia. The need for self-glorification comes from the displaced ego, and listlessness, or boredom, which gives us the seemingly endless hours in which to let our thoughts wander and obsess about such things. Instead of keeping the mind positively occupied with the good things of God, we start to daydream about ourselves in imaginary situations both good and bad. We start to think of ourselves as successful, famous, or exalted at this or that situation. We also fantasize about what we would do to people known or unknown if they were to challenge our self-esteem or success. It all starts with the thoughts. But thoughts eventually become words and actions. And I say, if you want to find out where your heart is, then see where your mind goes when it wanders. This is an interesting and often a most sobering exercise.

The list of eight thoughts begins with the small sensual sins such as gluttony. This leads to greater sensual sins such as sexual sin. Avarice is the need to possess and control material things, our own opinions and ideas, and other people and relationships. When we do not get the food we want, the sex we want, or the control we want, then we get angry. When anger is not healed through forgiveness and letting go of egoism, then we just get bitter. This poisons everything that we are and every relationship in our lives. One of those great poisons is acedia, or the noonday devil, often called listlessness or boredom. It was considered the greatest temptation for the solitary monk in the ancient desert because it causes one to allow thoughts to wander and obsess about all sorts of things. Self-esteem or self-glory is the need for small personal glory to stroke our displaced ego. When self-glory is not healed through humbly letting go of that ego, then we fall into the fully deadly sin of pride.

All of these have to do with letting go of the displaced ego. I am reminded of the old Campus Crusade for Christ tract about the right place for ego and Christ. Ego is necessary for any sense of consciousness. Ego is not bad when in the right place. The trouble is that we allow ego to sit on the throne of our life, while we place God and spirituality at the foot of the throne. Notice that in this bad use of ego God is still part of our life. But he is not on the throne either. This is a common mistake with religious people. When we let the old egoism die with Christ, then we can allow Jesus back on the throne of our lives, and the ego can take its right place at the foot of the throne. Ego can never disappear, or we would have no sense of self-consciousness. But it must exist in its right place. Ego should always remain at the foot of the throne, not on the throne. And Jesus must remain clearly on the throne of our life.

Envy is about wanting for ourselves the things that rightly only belong to God, and to whomever he chooses to give them. He gives good gifts to all. But when we allow the ego to control us, then we are not satisfied with what God has given us, and we want more and more for ourselves. When we do not get what we want, we begin to envy the goodness in others. This leads to resentment and anger. In effect, this is really envying God. This takes us right back to the first sin of humanity. We want to be God. This is blasphemy at its very core.

St. Benedict says that we are to see Christ in our spiritual leaders. I believe this is practice for something greater. Scripture teaches that we are to see Jesus in everyone, especially in the body of Christ. Jesus says, "Truly, I say to you, as you did it to one of the least of these my brethren, you did it to me" (Matt. 25:40). This means that when we envy the goodness God has given others, we do violence to seeing Jesus in others. This is also committing the sin of blasphemy.

St. Benedict also says we are to be obedient, not only to spiritual leaders and elders, but to all the brothers, and listen to the voice of the Holy Spirit not only through our leaders but even in the novices. St. Francis pretty much says the same thing. Both Benedict and Francis are fleshing out in a specific community dedicated to an intensive gospel way of life the teaching of Jesus himself.

Are we envious of others? If so, we are still functioning with ego on the throne of our lives. Let the displaced ego, the old and false self, die with Christ. Then we can be born again and raised up in Christ a new person where Jesus is on the throne of our life, and our ego is found at the foot of the throne. This is the place where it functions best.

Admonition 9
Charity

ST. FRANCIS WROTE:

Our Lord says in the Gospel, "Love your enemies" (Matt. 5:44). A person truly loves his enemy when he is not offended by the injury done to himself, but for love of God feels burning sorrow for the sin his enemy has brought on his own soul and proves his love in a practical way.

This is easy to say, but hard to do. I have been blessed with success in my life beyond what I could have ever imagined. Many have "praised me for all my success" (Ps. 49:19 Grail). Yet I have also had detractors. Most of these are distant, so remain largely impersonal to me. This goes with any public ministry. But some are up close and personal. Some have openly accused and attacked me or done so behind my back. I must confess that while I am rather resigned to this, and often passive about it, there is a part of me that's offended when I'm attacked. This can lead to classical passive/aggressive patterns that are destructive. Only later in life have I actually discovered what it is to love my enemies. I have also been gifted to have been able to reconcile with most of my enemies, though some remain unreachable. This saddens me and causes me to do penance for my part in the break.

What is love? We know "God is love" (1 John 4:8). St. John of the Cross said that all we will be asked when we die is, "How well have you loved?" The Trinity, the incarnation of the Word in Jesus Christ, the paschal mystery of the cross and resurrection, the church and all the sacraments are included in a correct understanding of love. The church herself only exists for love. Love is the complete emptying of self for the sake of another. It is the very nature of God. It is manifested most clearly in the dying of Jesus for God the Father, and for each of us personally. "Greater love has no man than this, that a man lay down his life for his friends" (John 15:13). Jesus is the greatest manifestation of the love of God for us, and for each of us personally. But how do *we* love? Jesus and the Bible give us plenty of helpful descriptions.

First Corinthians 13 gives the classical Christian description of love. "Love is patient and kind; love is not jealous or boastful," and so on. Jesus's Sermon on the Mount teaches what love looks like, and the purity of the attitudes and actions that come from real love. But how do we get there? How do we become capable of such love? Through self-emptying.

St. Paul's Letter to the Philippians says,

> Have this mind among yourselves, which was in Christ Jesus, who, though he was in the form of God, did not count equality with God a thing to be grasped, but emptied himself, taking the form of a servant, being born in the likeness of men. And being found in human form he humbled himself and became obedient unto death, even death on a cross. Therefore God has highly exalted him and bestowed on him the name which is above every name, that at the name of Jesus every knee should bow, in heaven and on earth and under the earth, and every tongue confess that Jesus Christ is Lord, to the glory of God the Father. (Phil. 2:5–11)

Love means the complete emptying the self for the sake of another. The greatest expression of love is in Jesus's self-emptying in his incarnation as God taking on humanity, and the passion of his death on the cross and rising from the dead. It is why renouncing or dying to the old self is so central to the teaching of both Jesus and St. Paul, his great disciple and apostle.

When the ego is still on the throne of our life, then we are easily offended. When the ego wants something and doesn't get it, it gets hurt and angry. Especially when we want recognition, good treatment, or even some appreciation— any time we don't receive what we think we are owed— we easily get offended. The trouble is that our definition of what is good and proper is often distorted when ego is driving our life. When the ego is at the foot of the throne where God rightly resides, we are not easily offended. There is nothing to offend.

When the ego is "sticking out" in places where it is not supposed to be, then we easily get our ego stepped on by others. So our taking "offense" is because we are out of order. It is not so much a matter of the behavior of others. That is between them and God. In the final analysis it is our problem, not theirs.

One great problem in relationships today is that we try to address the bad behavior of others, or the injustices of the world, before we have dealt with our own. When we do this before we at least substantially empty ourselves of the disordered self, then our definition of goodness or justice is often based on our own ego needs. Even when we get the definitions right, our methods of approaching others may still be ego driven. We want everyone to agree with us. We want our ego stroked. This is not real love.

Jesus clearly teaches,

> Judge not, that you be not judged. For with the judgment
> you pronounce you will be judged, and the measure you
> give will be the measure you get. Why do you see the
> speck that is in your brother's eye, but do not notice the
> log that is in your own eye? Or how can you say to your
> brother, 'Let me take the speck out of your eye,' when
> there is the log in your own eye? You hypocrite, first take
> the log out of your own eye, and then you will see clearly
> to take the speck out of your brother's eye. (Matt. 7:1-5)

This is countercultural to our modern culture, or probably
to any culture in human history.

This is most evident in our highly angry and polarized
political and social environment today. We hold others to
impossibly high standards of perfection; we judge them harshly
when they fail to meet those standards; and we expect, and
even demand understanding, forgiveness, and permission to
continue regarding our own sins, often blaming someone, or
something, else for them all the while.

This can even be true in religious matters. When the ego
is still in control we want to control what others think about
God, and we still try to arrange the church or our community
or ministry according to our opinions and agendas. This is
because deep down we really are still trying to be God, and we
try to conform the entire church and the world to our image,
instead of to God's. We think that we will finally have peace
when we get everyone to agree with us about God and Jesus.
But this is a model doomed to fail.

But when we really let go of the old self, we can let God
be God. Then we can address these things without the inner
need to have our own ego justified in changing other people's
minds to agree with us about religious matters. Many a pastor,

preacher, or teacher has mistaken a desire to get others to believe just like we do for a godly desire to bring the good news of Jesus Christ to others out of pure love. This is a most treacherous trap for religious people.

Some might mistake letting go of the displaced ego as retreating into a passive posture all the time. This is not so. And if we try this we eventually become classically passive-aggressive. We seem still and peaceful on the surface, but inwardly we are agitated and angry, like a volcano just waiting to blow.

There is a genuine passive dimension as we learn to silence our ego and pride and let go of our old patterns of behavior and relationships. This runs deep. But once this begins to take effect we can more easily flow back out into an activity that is healthy and life-giving to others. Indeed, it is an obligation.

Real love is self-emptying and self-diffusive. It flows outward in ways that really help other people. As St. Paul says of speech, we must say only the good things people really need to hear. The word he uses is "edifying" (Eph. 4:29). The Greek word for edification comes from *oikos*, "house," and *doma*, "build" or "roof," like a "dome." It means to "build up," like building an "edifice." St. Paul is telling us to speak only to build up another person, never to tear down or build up ourselves.

When we are still ego-driven our "charity" remains an attempt to gain recognition or to control others. It is incomplete at best and false at worst. Either way, it is an illusion that leads us into delusion if left unchecked. Such illusion and delusion are not from God. Real charity gives what is really needed for the genuine benefit of others. It has little to do with us. It is all about them and God. We are just instruments. But more than just an obligation that we must do, charity is simply a part of the nature of selfless love that we naturally do. It is a natural flow, like water flowing through an aqueduct from the reservoir of God's love to others.

St. Bernard of Clairvaux said that contemplative life is like a dam that stops the wild flow of water, or perhaps even a small trickle, and creates a reservoir through stillness. But it also builds up positive energy. It must eventually be released. St. Dominic expanded on this and said that ministry is like an aqueduct that channels the water of the reservoir with newfound power and direction. So we must first pray in deep contemplation and stillness to collect grace, and then become aqueducts of grace through ministry. It becomes almost second nature. As God simply is, so this kind of love simply *is* in those who love. If we really love, then we must share that love with others for the sake of others. This is done through words and actions. We empty ourselves for the sake of others.

Most of us know people who are like this. Some are monks and nuns, or other consecrated sisters and brothers. Others are just regular folks. One of the friends of our monastery is a "tree man." He is an expert in trees and is hired by people all around the wooded Ozarks of our area to help with the care of mother earth. But he is also known as just one of the nicest guys you can find. He helps us at the monastery. In fact, he doesn't just help us, he helps everyone, and is loved by our little town. He is a saint in the making in our midst. He is a man of love.

We only find our real self by completely letting go of self for the sake of others out of love. As Jesus clearly says, "He who finds his life will lose it, and he who loses his life for my sake will find it" (Matt. 10:39). This is the message of St. Francis because it is the central message of Jesus Christ.

Admonition 10
Exterior Mortification

ST. FRANCIS WROTE:
Many people blame the devil or their neighbor when they fall into sin or are offended. But that is not right. Everyone has his own enemy in his power and this enemy is his lower nature, which leads him into sin. Blessed are the servants of God who keep this enemy a prisoner under their control and protect themselves against it. As long as they do this, no other enemy, visible or invisible, can harm them.

We live in a culture of blame. We love to blame others for our problems. But we also want to be forgiven much, and we often call it abusive or hateful when others simply express their opinion about what we do.

We create laws, protocols, and rules that are often more burdensome than they are helpful, whether in our secular lives or in our lives of faith. Churches often err when they try to fill what is a moral void in the secular world with legislation. It works minimally, but it can never satisfy the need for real moral and spiritual vitality and health. Recently, Pope Francis has decried the rigidity of ritualistic legalists as "heretical" to authentic Catholicism. He calls them neo-Pelagianists, or those who think they can win their way to God through works. Radical language indeed, but it gets the point across clearly!

Instead of blaming the devil or our neighbor for the problems in our faith, what we need is revival. We need authentic Catholic revival. Beyond the rather obvious need for reform after sex scandals, liturgies are often lukewarm, and people are leaving churches because of it. We really only need three things to regain the attention of the people who are leaving the Church at an astounding rate: (1) better music and participation, (2) better preaching, and (3) a personal encounter with Jesus Christ in every Eucharist. And that's only the beginning.

The Pew Forum has recently identified three things Americans seek when seeking a church: (1) good preaching, (2) accessible and friendly leaders, and (3) a good worship experience. These things are fairly easy to achieve for those willing to make changes. I would add, we also need bishops and pastors who are true shepherds, not lords or CEOs. Most of our spiritual leaders begin humble of heart, but then sometimes they lose their humility along the way. Our shepherds need to be humble people who live on the same level as the flock they shepherd; I'd love to see them more truly accessible to their flock, dressed as they dress, talking as they talk, and visiting their homes as humble servants of God. I believe they would regain the respect and support of their flock, and perhaps the world. Fr. Joseph Ratzinger once prophesied in a radio interview (in 1969) that the church in the West might soon become much smaller, lose its secular power and prestige, and begin to meet in homes for liturgy and fellowship. He speculated that then we might discover what it is to be truly Christian again. I tend to agree.

Real spiritual revival changes lives. But unless that revival translates to our personal lifestyle it remains a sham. Even the most secular people can see through us. Throughout history, real revival has had profound social effects. The freeing of the slaves in America happened because there was a Spirit-led Great Awakening that swept America and Europe. This awakening changed the way people thought and lived. The Franciscan revival in thirteenth-century Europe brought a peace movement that disarmed the fighting factions of each city-state and region. In the early church, the appreciation of women brought forth a women's movement that greatly reduced both prostitution and abortion. These are just three examples, but I could go on and on. Earlier generations were not perfect, God knows, but these were instances when giant steps forward were taken in the spiritual and moral development of the human race, and of civilization.

Change is scary. It means stepping out from what we have settled for throughout most of life into becoming a new creation in Christ. It means letting the old self die through the cross of Christ so that we might truly be reborn in Christ. Most of us have settled for a version of ourselves that is not the person Jesus created us to be when we were conceived in our mother's womb. It's not that the self that we have settled for is necessarily wrong, but it is incomplete. Sometimes it is just flat-out sinful and wrong. We have to let the old disordered and incomplete self completely, or at least substantially, die so that we might be born again in Christ. And while there are certainly conversion points in our life, this does not happen just once. It happens every day. It happens at every Mass. It happens with every breath we breathe.

Change means stepping out of the boat of who and what we have settled for in the past. Stepping out of the boat is scary. It's like when St. Peter stepped out to walk on the water with Christ. I'm sure Peter didn't understand how to walk on water. He simply trusted and stepped out because Jesus called him to do so. Suddenly, he was walking on water! Then doubt took over. He took his eyes off Jesus, looked at the storm, and began to sink. Jesus reached out and pulled him up. Then he asked, "O man of little faith, why did you doubt?" (Matt. 14:31).

The Greek for "miracle" is *dynamis*. It's where we get the English word *dynamite*. It also translates as "power." It is used when speaking of the power of the Holy Spirit in Scripture. How do we receive miracles? By faith! Jesus says, "Have faith in God. Truly, I say to you, whoever says to this mountain, 'Be taken up and cast into the sea,' and does not doubt in his heart, but believes that what he says will come to pass, it will be done for him. Therefore I tell you, whatever you ask in prayer, believe that you receive it, and you will" (Mk. 11:23–24).

And what is faith? Hebrews says, "Now faith is the assurance of things hoped for, the conviction of things not seen" (Heb. 11:1). The Greek word for assurance is *hypostasis*. It is the word used by St. Cyril of Alexandria for the one "person" and the two *physeis* ("natures," where we get *physical*), or divine and human natures of Jesus Christ. It is also used of the persons of the Trinity. So it means that faith is the "personification" in the present of things we only hope for in the future. It literally *personifies miracles*!

Why don't we see miracles today? I think it's because we are just too rational. In Africa, we are seeing stunning revival. Miracles are happening. Six million Muslims converted to Christianity in one year alone. Over the last decade, Jesus has been appearing in the dreams of ISIS leaders, and former leaders, and they are converting to Christianity. They see miracles and even see people raised from the dead regularly. Why? Because they have not succumbed to rationalistic ideals and can still believe. Don't misunderstand me: we need rational minds. But rationalism limits us to a small understanding of the cosmos and of God. Both are very, very big, and we understand very, very little.

Jesus is asking us to step out of the boats of our safety zones. Where have you and I settled for something less that Jesus wills for us? Where are we still frustrated and angry? Where have we begun to blame others for our unwillingness to really change? Let's step out of the boat and walk on water with Jesus. Don't look at the troubles and storms of this world. Keep your eyes on Jesus, and you will not sink. But if you do, Jesus will reach to you under the waves to pull you back up again. All you have to do is reach up to Christ. Reach up to him now. Grab his hand. Don't blame others. Take the step and reach out to Jesus yourself. He will empower you to walk on water with him, and your life will become a walking miracle!

This is why St. Francis mentions "mortification" in this Admonition. Mortification means "being put to death." I am not good with mortification. I tried, in the beginning. I wanted to fast and keep vigil and the whole nine yards, although I stopped short at the "discipline"—the scourging of oneself that you've perhaps read about or seen in movies. Some of my post-Vatican II teachers said that life itself has enough opportunity for mortification, through the hardships we inevitably face. As I've gotten older I've discovered some truth to their cautions. But I have also recently again embraced the disciplined diet and sleep of fasting and vigils. When kept in moderation, and not going to an extreme, these have proved helpful to my spiritual life. The logic is simple: If I can't control even the simplest desires of the flesh for food and sleep, how can I control the deeper urges of carnality and ego?

St. Paul describes real Christian mortification when he says, "Put to death therefore what is earthly in you: immorality, impurity, passion, evil desire, and covetousness, which is idolatry. . . . But now put them all away: anger, wrath, malice, slander, and foul talk from your mouth. Do not lie to one another, seeing that you have put off the old nature with its practices and have put on the new nature, which is being renewed in knowledge after the image of its creator" (Col. 3: 5–10). This is a mortification that brings life, not death. Jesus says, "I came that they may have life, and have it abundantly" (John 10:19). When we surrender to Jesus we are not taken prisoner, and held captive, tortured, and made to accept things we do not believe. When we surrender to Jesus, we are set free, maybe for the first time in our life. Or maybe just for the first time in a long time, or even the first time today.

External mortification never merits grace on its own. It can, however, *cooperate* with grace, and *facilitate* its increase in our life. We have all met people who are addicted to religiosity. They are obsessed with rules, regulations, and rubrics. These things are good when used rightly, but they can be deadly when used wrongly. St. Francis warns us against this. This is why St. Paul says, "The written code kills, but the Spirit gives life" (2 Cor. 3:6).

It is good to have fundamentals, but we are not to be fundamentalists. It is good to conserve the apostolic traditions, but we are not to be neo- and arch-conservatives. It is good to liberally apply the gospel of Jesus Christ to all people, but we are not to be ironically closed-minded liberals who are accepting of everyone until others voice an opinion other than their own narrow secularist ideology. This reality rears its ugly head under many external forms. But inwardly it is the same "wolf in sheep's clothing" wherever it appears.

Aquinas said that we must do "the right thing rightly." Isn't it interesting how using the right thing wrongly achieves wrong results? Most of religion is a gift from God meant to lead us back to God. But when we make a god out of the gifts of God, they can lead us away from God. Religion is like a road sign to lead us to our destination. It is a map for the spiritual journey. But when we spend all our time with our heads buried in the map, we can miss the turnoff. Plus, we don't get to really enjoy the journey. So using the good gift of God badly can actually keep us from the very God the good gift was meant to lead us to! But using the good gift of God rightly is a sure aid in leading us into full communion with God and his church.

Effective steps of mortification in our lives begin with the way we think. Jesus says, "But what comes out of the mouth proceeds from the heart, and this defiles a man. For out of the heart come evil thoughts, murder, adultery, fornication, theft, false witness, slander. These are what defile a man" (Matt. 15:18–20). We are to have the "mind of Christ" (1 Cor. 2:16). How? The Holy Spirit brings to mind all that Jesus said. It is supernatural, and only those who have experienced it know what this really is. All others are left on the outside looking in. But it takes some cooperation with grace. We must read the word of God in Scripture, and specifically the teachings of Jesus Christ. When we do so it "quickens," or energizes, the words of Scripture within us as we read them. Words that used to seem far off, or obscure, now make sense. This is because it is now Jesus within us through the Spirit who recognizes his own words! That is why the person of God "meditates day and night" on Scripture (Ps. 1:2). That is why one paraphrase of Proverbs 16:9 is that "we are what we think." If we think good thoughts, we will say and do good things. If we repeatedly turn over negative thoughts, we will eventually turn to sin. How do we fill our minds with positive thoughts?

One good way is to read Scripture or the writings of the saints or church teaching. We must set aside time every day to read a bit of Scripture. A great place to start is with the readings of the day at Mass, or the Liturgy of the Hours.

We must use the mind to visualize what we read. St. Bonaventure says, "Imagination assists understanding." Even mathematical thinking involves seeing the numbers and geometric figures and shapes in the mind. This is not speed-reading, where we breeze through entire sentences of paragraphs to pass a test or exam. In meditation, we take time to see and imagine Jesus and the disciples feeding the multitudes, or performing miracles, and so on.

Then we allow this meditation to become a prayer. It is a living dialogue with God that encompasses our entire being. We are no longer just reading, or meditating within ourselves, but reaching to and dialoguing with God, who is within and without us, in a living relationship of love that is personal, intimate, and life-changing.

Finally, hopefully, we pass over into contemplation. Here we simply learn how to be with the One Who Is. It uses, includes, and surpasses all senses, thoughts, ideas, or emotions. Like a man and woman who bask in afterglow after full union, or like two friends who know how to just sit with one another, we simply enjoy being in God's presence. The first three stages are more active, and they set the stage for contemplation. But they cannot force it. Contemplation emerges on its own in God's good time. Traditionally the first three stages are called the "active life," and the fourth is called the "contemplative life."

Active life includes traditional means of asceticism, devotion, prayer, and works of mercy. Are we getting stuck in the externals of our faith? Are we operating in the life of the Spirit? If not, do not despair. Seek the guidance of God, the presence of God's Holy Spirit in your life, and then—as St. Francis reminds us—the external practices of our faith will come to life.

Admonition 11

No One Should Be Scandalized at Another's Fall

ST. FRANCIS WROTE:

Nothing should upset a servant of God except sin. And even then, no matter what kind of sin has been committed, if he is upset or angry for any other reason except charity, he is only drawing blame upon himself. A servant of God lives a good life and avoids sin when he is never angry or disturbed at anything. Blessed is the person who keeps nothing for himself, but renders "to Caesar the things that are Caesar's, and to God the things that are God's" (Matt. 22:21).

This is a tough one. We get upset by sin, but it is usually another person's sin, not our own. And we often walk around agitated, frustrated, and angry about the external circumstances of our life. This is not the way to the love, joy, and peace of Jesus Christ.

As a monastic superior, I have thought at times that the monastery would run just fine if everyone would just stop sinning and do what I asked them to do! Worse yet, I have sometimes found my thoughts preoccupied with why "they" can't just do things right. I have obsessed about other people's problems. Then I'm reminded of the old Billy Graham saying, "If you find a perfect church, don't join it, or you'll ruin it!" The problem is seldom with others, though others will always sin. The problem is with me. If I want to change the world, I must begin with myself. Blaming others is a devil's trick.

Jesus says, "Peace I leave with you; my peace I give to you; not as the world gives do I give to you. Let not your hearts be troubled, neither let them be afraid" (John 14:27). This does not mean worldly peace. It means a peace that is with us even in the middle of chaos, agitation, and war. It is a peace that passes understanding. As St. Paul writes to the Philippians, "And the peace of God, which passes all understanding, will keep your hearts and your minds in Christ Jesus" (Phil. 4:7).

For St. Francis, as a radical disciple of Jesus, this peace comes primarily from the power of the Holy Spirit within, not from external circumstances. St. Paul calls this a fruit of the Holy Spirit. He says, "But the fruit of the Spirit is love, joy, peace" (Gal. 5:23). This peace is not found by getting all the external things of our life to align perfectly with what we think should be going on in our ministry, community, local parish, church, or world. While we do our best to find external peace to some degree, such external hopes are futile. Ultimately, they lead to frustration, then to anger and bitterness, which paves the way to all manner of negativity in our life.

The peace of Jesus is a work of the Holy Spirit. St. Paul says that the fruit of the Spirit appear in our life as we have "crucified the flesh with its passions and desires." He says,

And those who belong to Christ Jesus have crucified the
flesh with its passions and desires.
If we live by the Spirit, let us also walk by the Spirit.
(Gal. 5:24–25)

As we bring the old self to the cross of Jesus and let it die,
the power of the Holy Spirit, who is already given to us in so
many ways, emerges and operates fully.

Anger is also mentioned in this Admonition. Jesus teaches
against anger when he says in the Sermon on the Mount, "You
have heard that it was said to the men of old, 'You shall not
kill; and whoever kills shall be liable to judgment.' But I say to
you that every one who is angry with his brother shall be liable
to judgment; whoever insults his brother shall be liable to the
council, and whoever says, 'You fool!' shall be liable to the hell
of fire" (Matt. 5:21–22).

There is a godly anger. Psalm 4 says, "Be angry, but sin not;
commune with your own hearts on your beds, and be silent"
(Ps. 4:4). But notice: this implies a silence and peace in the
midst of anger.

Clearly, Jesus was upset when he overturned the money-
changer's tables in Matthew 21:12–13! Mark's Gospel indicates
that Jesus was sometimes even exasperated with his disciples
when they simply didn't "get it" (Mk. 6:52; 8:17). This is a godly
anger. But very little of our anger is godly. The book of James
warns, "Let every man be quick to hear, slow to speak, slow to
anger, for the anger of man does not work the righteousness of
God" (Jas. 1:19–20).

How do we cure anger? First, we cure the thoughts leading up
to it. We cure gluttony with moderate fasting, or eating simply
and frugally every day. We cure sexual sin by finding Jesus as
our primary Spouse; then all relationships flow chastely from
our personal love relationship with Jesus. Avarice is, at least
in in monastic tradition, cured by living in community with

others under a rule and a good abbot, or leader. For most of us it means living in the community of our family, local church, and workplace.

Anger is specifically cured through forgiveness. The biblical words for forgiveness mean to "divorce," or "send away," judgment for sin. As far as the east is from the west, so does God cast away sin through forgiveness (Ps. 103:12). Jesus teaches us all forgiveness in the Our Father. "And forgive us our debts, As we also have forgiven our debtors" (Matt. 6:12). Forgiveness runs like a river of peace and grace through the teachings of Jesus in every Gospel account. Forgiveness also binds and looses sin in ourselves and in others.

We are all called to forgive sins. When we judge or bind, we not only bind others, we bind ourselves. The person caught in the need to judge everyone and everything certainly binds up those around them. This also looses darkness and sin. We see this in monastic community. One unforgiving monastic can spread a wet blanket over an entire community without saying a word. But the saddest thing is that unforgiveness not only binds others, it also binds up the full working of the Holy Spirit in the person doing the judging. Sin is loosed, and the person goes from bad to worse, ending up in a living hell right here on earth.

St. Francis gives us a way out through forgiveness. In his "Letter to a Minister," he says that there is no religious in the entire world, no matter how far they have fallen, who could not be called back to forgiveness simply by looking into a leader's eyes. Wow! This is always stunning to me. The eyes are the windows to the soul. If we have the peace of the Spirit within, then we call everyone we see to that peace. If we are forgiven, then we call everyone to forgiveness.

The balance of forgiveness and upholding righteousness often confuses many people. It is understandably difficult to balance these two things. Forgiving sin does not mean ignoring sin. Nor does upholding the truth of righteousness and sin mean constantly judging those who do not conform to our idea of righteousness.

Jesus shows us the way in the Gospel of St. John with the woman caught in the very act of adultery. After saying that those who are without sin should cast the first stone, and everyone has laid down their stones, Jesus says, "Neither do I condemn you; go, and do not sin again" (John 8:11). He forgives her, but does not condone her adultery, and calls her to genuine repentance and change to a better way of life. Judgment doesn't allow people to change. Forgiveness releases repentance into a person's life. Righteousness follows.

But upholding righteousness doesn't mean judging everyone and everything all the time. We must forgive, or judgment will give way to frustration, and then to an anger that eats us up inside.

Some say that we should only forgive when others repent and come back to righteousness, as we understand it. There is ample evidence in Scripture to support the activation of forgiveness upon repentance. But even then, Jesus challenges us regarding repeated sins. "Take heed to yourselves; if your brother sins, rebuke him, and if he repents, forgive him; and if he sins against you seven times in the day, and turns to you seven times, and says, 'I repent,' you must forgive him" (Luke 17:3–4).

Making forgiveness conditional on the part of the one doing the forgiving remains a flawed practice in pastoral experience. First, our understanding of righteousness and sin isn't always that of God. Only God can judge a human soul. Second, when we withhold forgiveness in our heart, that is harmful for us. It not only binds other people through a bad spirit, but it also binds us up. So we must have a loving heart and forgiving spirit that invites others to mercy and forgiveness. That is why St. Francis says that the eyes of the superior must always call a sinful brother back to forgiveness.

I often imagine that forgiveness and repentance are like a cup left out in the yard in the rain. The rain of grace and mercy is constantly falling. In order to collect the water it must be right side up. If it is upside down, then it must first "turn around," or repent, in order to collect the water of forgiveness and mercy. We must always call people, not to judgment and condemnation, but to forgiveness and mercy.

St. Francis, in this Admonition, as always, is pointing us back to Jesus and the gospel. Jesus teaches that forgiveness is the key to seeing miracles in our life. He says powerfully,

> Truly, I say to you, whoever says to this mountain, "Be taken up and cast into the sea," and does not doubt in his heart, but believes that what he says will come to pass, it will be done for him. Therefore I tell you, whatever you ask in prayer, believe that you receive it, and you will. And whenever you stand praying, forgive, if you have anything against any one; so that your Father also who is in heaven may forgive you your trespasses. (Mk. 11:23–25)

Admonition 12
How to Know the Spirit of God

St. Francis wrote:

We can be sure that a person is a true servant of God and has the spirit of God if their lower nature does not give way to pride when God accomplishes some good through them, and if they seem all the more worthless and inferior to others in their own eyes. Our lower nature is opposed to every good.

Like some of the others, this is a shockingly direct and short Admonition. St. Francis says that this is the test of how we know whether we really are walking in the Spirit of God: if we don't give way to pride when God begins to accomplish good things through us. He isn't referring to spiritual gifts (1 Cor. 12–14) or powerful manifestations of power, miracles, healing, and deliverance. He is talking about simple good works. He is referring to personal sanctification.

What Francis is talking about is the fruit of the Spirit—for our personal sanctification, or holiness that builds good character. Paul says,

But the fruit of the Spirit is love, joy, peace, patience, kindness, goodness, faithfulness, gentleness, self-control; against such there is no law. And those who belong to Christ Jesus have crucified the flesh with its passions and desires.

If we live by the Spirit, let us also walk by the Spirit. (Gal. 5:22–25).

Jesus says that we know good and evil people by their fruit (Matt. 12:33).

So it is not enough to claim to have the Spirit of God, to be enthusiastic, or to get all our liturgical rubrics right. These things are all good. But, as Thomas Aquinas says, we must "do the right thing rightly." We must do the Jesus thing in the Jesus way to really accomplish the will of God in Jesus Christ. He says, "Not every one who says to me, 'Lord, Lord,' shall enter the kingdom of heaven, but he who does the will of my Father who is in heaven. On that day many will say to me, 'Lord, Lord, did we not prophesy in your name, and cast out demons in your name, and do many mighty works in your name?' And then will I declare to them, 'I never knew you; depart from me, you evildoers'" (Matt. 7:21–23). Externals are not enough for our personal salvation.

Diodochus of Photiki, a bishop of the fifth century in Macedonia, said that we receive two anointings of the Spirit: One for personal salvation and sanctification, and another for ministry. When anointed for ministry we cannot enter fully into the anointing for personal salvation, or all we could do is weep tears of repentance and joy. When in ministry God removes us temporarily from the full weight of this anointing so we might minister to others.

I am a Catholic Charismatic. I love charismatic expressions. I also love the contemplative aspects of the Franciscan, monastic, and especially the desert tradition of the Christian East. I first experienced the gift of tongues on an airplane. I had heard of this gift since my involvement with the Jesus Movement, but hadn't personally experienced it. I was flying to California to meet with my brother, Terry, for a music project around the time of the Talbot Brothers recording on Warner Brothers (1972). I was casually looking out the window praising God in my thoughts and heart for the beauty of the clouds and the earth below. I kind of went out of myself in praise, and I recall coming out of it quietly speaking words that weren't part of any language I knew of. I remember the guy next to me looking at me strangely, so I stopped before it got very loud.

Since that time, I have experienced the gift of tongues in countless prayer meetings in parishes, conventions, and at our monastery. I have found the gift a real way to open up to nonconceptual praise and thanks beyond the limits of human understanding. Later, I would find the same thing in contemplative prayer beyond thoughts, words, or emotions. Both have opened my spiritual life up in ways that mere ideas and concepts simply cannot.

I also know that the apostles needed more than a personal experience of the incarnate Word in Jesus to empower their life in Christ. They had heard every sermon he preached, seen every miracle he worked. They had seen him be true to his own teaching on love to the point of death on a cross. They had even seen him resurrected and ascended! But Jesus said that they didn't have what they needed yet. They had to wait in Jerusalem for the power from on high before they could be fully equipped for both ministry and personal perseverance as his apostles and disciples. That empowerment came at Pentecost with the charismatic gift of tongues. Other gifts soon followed.

I'm also aware that sometimes those who most openly manifest charismatic gifts in public can be the least Christlike in daily life. That's why we have New Testament lists of gifts of the Spirit that are more extrinsically related to ministry, and a list of the fruit of the Spirit intrinsically related to one's character. Perhaps that's also why the church has opted for emphasis on the Hebrew Scripture list found in Isaiah 11.

How does St. Francis describe this lifestyle and attitude test of the Holy Spirit? He says, "If their lower nature does not give way to pride when God accomplishes some good through them, and if they seem all the more worthless and inferior to others in their own eyes." This Admonition is related to the former one on blaming others. The ego, or the old self (Rom. 6:6), wants to be praised and noticed in all things, and gives way to pride. It claims for itself what should rightly be offered back to God.

We need self-worth and a healthy self-esteem. We are created and redeemed in Christ. We are to anticipate one another in showing honor and respect (Rom. 12:19), and give honor to whom honor is due (Rom. 13:7). But we are not to seek them without recognizing that all good things ultimately come from God and lead back to God. Without being remade in Christ, these legitimate things easily fall into pride and our wanting to keep for ourselves what rightly belongs to God. Seemingly small, harmless things can grow into something worse. First, we claim glory for ourselves in little things, then we begin claiming it in bigger things. If left unchecked, little needs for self-glory give birth to full-on pride. St. Francis teaches that the only thing we can really claim ownership to is our sin.

All good things come from God and flow back to God. Our very self is made in the image and likeness of God. Since we lost the likeness of God though sin, our redemption is accomplished through the love of God poured out through the shed blood of Jesus Christ. Jesus gives us the Holy Spirit—a gift, a grace of God. Spiritual gifts then come from God, and our ministries come from the Holy Spirit. So why do we think we possess them?

Our sin alone is ours. Sin has no creative power. It is always a perversion of righteousness. It distorts something holy into something unholy. Think of it: lust is a perversion of love; avarice a perversion of stewardship; and egoism is a perversion of legitimate self-awareness when the ego, or self, is rightly situated in Christ. Sin has no real creative power. It can only pervert the good.

This brings us to humility. Etymologically, "humility" in the Greek means being brought to the earth, or being brought low.

A Carthusian prior at St. Hugh's Charterhouse in Parkminster, England, once said to me, "Humility only happens through humiliation." Humility cannot be planned or neatly learned. It happens through unplanned challenges, crises, and even failures. These come unexpectedly, sometimes when we think everything is going our way and all is right with our world. Many people tell me that just when they think everything has lined up for final success and peace, disaster seems to strike, and all their well-laid plans come to nothing. The issue isn't whether these things will happen; in the course of life, they always do. The question is, how will we respond? Humiliation can either make us angry and bitter, poisoning everything in our lives, or we can allow it to humble us before people, creation, and God. That humility brings us back to truth.

St. Francis says, essentially, "Humility is the truth." It brings us back to the ground of ultimate reality. It is in that Reality, and that truth, that we can begin again. It is there that we can be born again. This happens most completely and powerfully through the cross and resurrection of Jesus Christ.

This truth is that we are created in the image and likeness of God (Gen. 1:26). When we sinned, or strayed from the path, God loved us so much that he sacrificed his Son to redeem us. Jesus shed every drop of blood for us all, and for each of us personally. This is stunning. God loves each of us that much! But this does not make us boastful or proud. It makes us humble, but also confident of God's love, not because of us, but because of him. Once we really realize this truth we can walk in godly boldness, but we simply cannot walk in arrogance or pride.

It is this thought that St. Francis emphasizes toward the end of this short Admonition: "They seem all the more worthless and inferior to others in their own eyes." St. Paul says, "Do nothing from selfishness or conceit, but in humility count others better than yourselves" (Phil. 2:3). This is not a form of feigned humility—which is always, ultimately, pride under the guise of humility. Nor is it masochism, which blasphemes the reality of our creation and redemption in Christ. It is walking in an immediate awareness of the truth of this Reality in God. It is humility in creation, sin and redemption, and confidence in redemption.

St. Francis then concludes by admitting, "Our lower nature is opposed to every good." The Scriptures tell us that we are to die to the old self and rise a new creation in Christ (2 Cor. 5:17). We are to throw off the deeds of darkness and "put on" the new person in Jesus (Rom. 13:14). Our baptism is the sacramental aid in this. But it must be stirred up daily through faith. Faith fully releases and activates the power of the Spirit, who empowers the gifts conferred in the sacraments. Baptism is the ground from which every other gift of the Spirit or state of life in the church flows. But that is only part of the story.

The monastic fathers and mothers tell us that the old self is like a spoiled child who throws a temper tantrum when denied what it is accustomed to habitually getting though sin. Our hunger, thirst, being hot or cold, and physical desires seem almost intolerable when we initially deny them through discipline in Christ. But they are only throwing a "temper tantrum." The same is true of our ego's need for praise or control.

Sin often feels good initially. Gluttony feels great until we get fat and sick from obesity. Sex is a lot of fun until we inherit the relational and physical complications of illicit practices and relationships. Avarice feels good until we are possessed by our possessions, consumed by what we consume, controlled by our need to control. Anger really feels great at first blush, but eventually it eats us up inside. Self-glory can feel good when we receive the affirmation we crave, but destroys us through frustration, anger, and bitterness that poisons all else in our life. And so it goes.

The old, unredeemed self always tries to rise back up to regain control of what it has lost through redemption in Christ. Unredeemed senses, thoughts, or feelings try to get their power back. This is what St. Francis ends this Admonition with: the irony that our senses, thoughts, and emotions are all more than satisfied when we let go of the old patterns that promised so much, but delivered so little. Old patterns enslaved us. Jesus sets us free!

Admonition 13
Patience

ST. FRANCIS WROTE:

"Blessed are the peacemakers, for they shall be called sons of God" (Matt. 5:9). We can never tell how patient or humble a person is when everything is going well with them. But when those who should cooperate with them do the exact opposite, then we can tell. A person has as much patience and humility as they have then, and no more.

One of my greatest downfalls is impatience. It's probably the weakness the people who know me best will confirm I need to work on. I am reminded of the old saying, "Lord, give me patience, and I want it now!" Perhaps you know what I mean. Sometimes we are even impatient with our impatience. I am not alone in this process. What St. Francis said is something similar. Again, this Admonition is short and sweet. It is simple, but it is far from simplistic!

It is said that a chain is only as strong as its weakest link. When the weak link snaps, the whole chain breaks. We are only as patient and humble as are when we are facing the unexpected challenges and conflicts of life. It's easy to imagine ourselves to be spiritual, peaceful, patient, and so on when everything is going well. But when things go badly we find out who we really are. It is always revelatory.

As St. Paul says, "When people say, 'There is peace and security,' then sudden destruction will come upon them as travail comes upon a woman with child, and there will be no escape" (1 Thess. 5:3). While this refers primarily to the time before the second coming of Christ, it also applies to his comings throughout our life. He often comes, not in the times of peace and safety, but in the challenging times of conflict and crises. Often it is there that he comes in full truth—either when we are either on our knees in humility or standing self-righteously in our pride.

There is no escaping times of unplanned setbacks, challenges, even tragedies. They happen to all of us. No life is immune from them. Certainly, the history of Christianity confirms that Christians are not immune from them. The question is how we will handle them when they come. This is the test of the authenticity of our discipleship in Jesus Christ.

Part of navigating this is learning how to face our tragedies with faith. Faith personifies in the present the things we only hope for in the future (Heb. 11:1). It looks beyond the things we see with the eyes to the things we see with our spirit. "We walk by faith, not by sight" (2 Cor. 5:7). It also sees not just sin but also potential righteousness through forgiveness. This transforms tragedy into triumph, turns defeats into victories, and redeems sin with righteousness. It does so by seeing not obstacles, but challenges. This strengthens faith and builds character. It empowers us to believe that all things are possible with God.

St. Francis illustrates this answer. We are told of the "perfect joy of St. Francis" in the early legends of his life. I will paraphrase the story here. Francis questions Brother Leo and asks him what perfect joy is. This is a rhetorical question. But then Francis says that it is not when Jesus works wonders, or we become great preachers and evangelists, or when we do great work for the poorest of the poor. He says that it is when we arrive at the door of our home or monastery after a long trip in the rain and the snow, and knock, cold, wet, tired, hungry, and exhausted; instead of being welcomed by our own community or family, we are turned away as strangers; we are refused entry. Even worse, to keep us from returning to try again, we are beaten bloody with a club, left broken and alone, and thrown into a snowdrift. St. Francis says that it is only then that we discover how much joy we really have in Christ. If we are to maintain our love, joy, and peace in this terrible rejection and persecution, then we really know the love, joy, and peace of the Spirit in Christ. If not, the love, joy, and peace we think we have is only superficial and fleeting. At best, it is incomplete. At worst, we are living in a delusion.

Now, most of us will not face anything as graphic or extreme as what St. Francis describes. But we will all eventually face some form of rejection from those from whom we seek acceptance. It might come from someone we have alienated, or an enemy. It might even come from a friend who isn't even aware that they have rejected or hurt us. It often even comes from those closest to us, someone we love. This is always most difficult.

Our immediate tendency is to say, "Hey! Why are you treating me that way?" We face rejection with rejection and anger with anger. It starts with surprise, then passes through frustration, and ends in anger. Anger ends in killed relationships with God, others, and even with ourselves. Anger always spills the blood of violence. It is either emotional or literal. We say that our anger is righteous or justified, because the treatment we receive often seems unwarranted, unjust, and unfair. But it goes much deeper!

As we have seen, the Eastern monastic tradition says that unhealed anger has a way of hiding inside the deepest recesses of our heart and soul. We live a life of little hurts and angry responses. But anger is exhausting, so we tend to let it go after a while. But it isn't gone. It's only hiding. When we don't really know how to heal anger by choosing forgiveness, it might recede into the dark corners of our heart, only to rear its ugly head when another conflict or affront to our self-esteem arises. When it does, it must be brought to the cross of Jesus Christ for complete healing. Only then can we really be raised up in his resurrection and born again in the Holy Spirit as a new person in Christ. Only then can we really be substantially free of that anger and hatred that so often imprison our soul. Jesus is the way out of that prison. Forgiveness is the key that unlocks the prison door. All we need to do is turn the key, let Jesus open the door, and walk out into real and lasting freedom.

St. Peter writes: "In this you rejoice, though now for a little while you may have to suffer various trials, so that the genuineness of your faith, more precious than gold which though perishable is tested by fire, may redound to praise and glory and honor at the revelation of Jesus Christ" (1 Pet. 1:6–7). And again: "But rejoice in so far as you share Christ's sufferings, that you may also rejoice and be glad when his glory is revealed" (1 Pet. 4:13).

The first Christians were persecuted and martyred cruelly, first by their own Jewish people, then by the Romans. Suffering has been our experience throughout history and around the world, but especially in the early days. It was an inescapable fact of life for those who would not renounce their faith in Jesus. They learned how to move through the suffering of that rejection and misunderstanding in the cross and resurrection of Jesus. They supernaturalized that suffering through the suffering and glorification of Jesus Christ and transformed it into a source of joy. Therefore, they were no longer angry or upset when they encountered it.

We can do the same today. We are facing a world that is increasingly hostile toward Christ and Christians. We can even face it in our families, and in our faith or religious communities. It requires a complete transformation of the way we think. We do this through prayer and meditation on God's Word, and the empowerment of the Spirit and the nourishment of the sacraments, especially the Eucharist.

What happens when we fail? We will, you know. We must humbly confess our shortcomings and confidently ask for and accept, but not presumptuously demand, forgiveness. This confession is both sacramental and personal with those with whom we have difficulties. St. John says, "If we say we have no sin, we deceive ourselves, and the truth is not in us. If we confess our sins, he is faithful and just, and will forgive our sins and cleanse us from all unrighteousness. If we say we have not sinned, we make him a liar, and his word is not in us" (1 John 1:8–10). This can be and is best done directly to God first and is then both confirmed and strengthened through the sacraments administered through God's valid ministers.

We should never let past sins keep us from forgiveness. Most of us have times of impatience and anger. This is part of the unregenerate human condition. But the good news is that Jesus sets us free. He does so directly through prayer, and through the ministry of mercy he has entrusted to the church. So I urge you, do not delay your confession, change of heart and mind, and new beginning in Christ. The Holy Spirit is saying that today, if you hear his voice, harden not your heart (Heb. 3:7–8).

Admonition 14
Poverty of Spirit

ST. FRANCIS WROTE:

"Blessed are the poor in spirit, for theirs is the kingdom of heaven" (Matt. 5:3). There are many people who spend all their time at their prayers and other religious exercises and mortify themselves by long fasts and so on. But if anyone says as much as a word that implies a reflection on their self-esteem or takes something from them, they are immediately up in arms and annoyed. These people are not really poor in spirit. A person is only poor in spirit if he hates himself and loves anyone who strikes him "on the cheek" (Matt. 5:39).

Again, St. Francis uses language that is almost unthinkable to the modern reader. Most of us have rarely, if ever, been slapped in the face. Such language should shock us enough to wake us up to the importance of this teaching.

Francis was a champion of gospel poverty. He is called the *Poverello*, or "little poor man." We might expect that this Admonition would have some reference to the poverty of Jesus, but it doesn't. It immediately goes deeper. It goes to the spirit of poverty. This Admonition is about gospel poverty. It addresses attitudes behind actions, not just actions—and it is surprisingly critical of Christian religious practices when those practices do not match the actual lifestyle of the person practicing. My experience in monastic community and ministry confirms the truth of this Admonition. We have all met people who are very religious, but not very Christian, and certainly not much like Jesus. They are most concerned about the color or cut of their religious habit; perhaps the use of rosaries, devotions, or liturgical rubrics; or some other external thing or rule. But they really aren't much like the Jesus or the saints who initiated those things. Some of the most religious people I know are the angriest, most judgmental, and most downright dysfunctional folks I have ever encountered! They are almost obsessive regarding liturgy and devotions, but often filled with an anger that stems from their rigid application of religion, and a rather constant judgment of others.

Yet some other religious people I regularly encounter seem to be true living saints. Religion has a way of bringing out both the best and the worst in individuals and humanity.

Francis is talking about bad religion on a simple, everyday level, something that is personal and practical in the daily life of a monastery, parish, or family. He is addressing the situation of the typical angry Christian. We have all encountered such people, or maybe we have been like this ourselves. Picture for a moment the monastic, parishioner, or family member who employs their religious practices with too much zeal, or to the point of unhealthy scrupulosity, or just to an absurdity immediately apparent to others but not to them. In the Jesus Movement, we used to call this "a religious spirit." They are always praying, but they have little time for real compassion. They often have other psychological issues that accompany these forms of religion. They are often obsessive-compulsive or passive-aggressive. Scrupulosity, rigidity, anger, and judgment toward themselves or others are often displayed at work or at home. These are not necessarily psychotic, which implies a break with reality. But they are often neurotic, which involves being overanxious or obsessive, or worrying and turning the mind overmuch. And let's be honest, most of us suffer from some little neurosis somewhere! Most of us carry some sort of unhealed anger.

Where does this anger come from? On the most basic level, it comes when we try to possess or control something, and don't get what we want. In the case of religion, we try to possess religion to achieve a reward, and we get angry when we don't get what we want. Sometimes we get angry with ourselves, and sometimes we get upset with others. Usually it is because we are looking at religion externally, and not discovering the inner empowerment of the Spirit.

This anger comes when we try to possess God instead of allowing God to possess us. When we try to possess the externals of religion we are enslaved to them rather than allowing their gracious use to free us up. When we allow the Spirit of God to really possess us, we are set free. When we surrender in the world we are taken captive, tortured, and made to say things we don't really believe. When we surrender in Jesus, we are set free. We get to share his victory maybe for the first time, or maybe for the first time in long time, or even the first time today. So, anger comes from possessiveness and ego attachment. Ironically, this can even involve the religion that is supposed to set us free from such possessiveness.

Scrupulosity comes from the Latin for "scruple," which means a pebble. Like a pebble caught on the inside of the sandal or shoe of our soul, it is small and almost unnoticeable, but can keep us from walking comfortably or running well. It is also that way with scrupulous religion. What begins as a conscientious attempt to do the right thing, please God, and help people can degenerate into something that hurts others and ourselves, and does not really accomplish the will of God.

It can cause us to stumble and fall. Sometimes we take a bad fall. But have no fear. We can always rise in Christ.

Some people advocate a complete jettisoning of all religion because of the bad fruit sometimes found in the bad exercise of it. This is, of course, not my position. I often hear megachurch pastors advertise on television with the hook: "We aren't religious. We are spiritual at our church." They make their message seem simple and easy, but really it is too simplistic. We need religion and spirituality, not just one or the other. Why?

Religion without spirituality is dead. It remains just theology and ritual that remains largely exterior to the human spirit and soul. But spirituality without religion is formless and has no real embodiment. Christianity is incarnational because Jesus himself was the Word incarnate, in "flesh," or *carne*. He is the Incarnation. Real Christianity is like Jesus, spirit in body, and divinity in humanity. As soon as spirituality takes some form on earth it is immediately a religion, whether we like it or not. Even those megachurches that claim to have no religion are a religion because they have some outer forms that express and strengthen their faith. So we need both. We need spirituality to enliven religion, and we need religion to give embodiment to spirituality.

I think of a dove, which must have two wings to fly. We need the wing of spirituality and the wing of religion in order for our spiritual life to truly soar to the heavens in the power of the Holy Spirit as followers of Jesus Christ, who was both human and divine, flesh and spirit.

Still, Jesus addresses some of his harshest words, not against sinners, but against overly religious people. He seems to get along quite well with prostitutes, and even tax collectors (who were considered the lowest of Jewish society because they were traitors to their own people by collecting taxes for the occupying Romans). But Jesus repeatedly upsets religious people, and they upset him. The very people who are supposed to be righteous upset him the most. They really upset him. "And he looked around at them with anger, grieved at their hardness of heart" (Mk. 3:5). He minces no words in upbraiding them.

When the externals of a religion we profess don't really work for us, we often proclaim it all the louder to try and make it work. We dig in deeper. Plus, the more we fail to live it, the more we demand that others should. Often it is those who are unfaithful and immoral privately who rail the loudest against faithlessness and immorality in others. But it's a sham. "Woe to you, scribes and Pharisees, hypocrites! for you tithe mint and dill and cummin, and have neglected the weightier matters of the law, justice and mercy and faith; these you ought to have done, without neglecting the others. You blind guides, straining out a gnat and swallowing a camel!" (Matt. 23:23–24). This is classic scrupulosity and hypocrisy as well.

The word *hypocrite* means "actor." It means putting on a show for others to feel better about ourselves, and is addressed in a couple of the above verses. When our inner spirituality is not working we often focus on the externals. Sometimes this is okay. It has been said that if you want to be holy, start acting holy, and it will eventually sink in. But this presumes that at some point real holiness will sink deeper into the spirit and soul of our life. When it doesn't sink deeper we start playing a game. We start acting. Soon the old self steps up, the ego sets in, and we begin to attach our identity to the external religious things we do. This is backward. Religious practices are supposed to take us deeper and assist us in releasing our ego attachments and false identities in externals by finding our identity in Christ. When they fail to do that they backfire, and they hurt the practitioner as much as anyone else.

Religion is a road map leading to our destination. Our destination is a personal encounter, or a love relationship with Christ, and full communion, or common union, in him with each other. Too many of us become obsessed with the road map. We spend too much time and attention with our nose in the map, and we miss the turnoff. Also, we never get to really enjoy the journey. Religion can free us or bring bondage. It can bind or loose either sin or the Spirit. So, what's the solution?

In this Admonition, St. Francis quotes Jesus in saying that we must love those who strike us in the face. He says, "A person is truly poor in spirit if he hates himself and loves anyone who strikes him 'on the cheek.'" Really? Yes. Learning how to actively love those who oppose us, who persecute us, and cause us physical harm is nothing short of stunning. It is simply beyond our fallen nature. All of us resist harm.

This is possible only by having a personal encounter with Jesus Christ, by dying to the old self and rising a new creation through his cross and resurrection, and through the power of the Holy Spirit in our lives. St. Paul said,

> Those who belong to Christ Jesus have crucified the flesh with its passions and desires.
> If we live by the Spirit, let us also walk by the Spirit. (Gal. 5:24–25)

Admonition 15
The Peacemakers

⌒ ST. FRANCIS WROTE:

"Blessed are the peacemakers, for they shall be called sons of God" (Matt. 5:9). They are truly peacemakers who are able to preserve their peace of mind and heart for love of our Lord Jesus Christ, despite all that they suffer in this world.

I like to think I'm a peaceful guy. I like to pray, be still, and be quiet. I'm essentially contemplative, though I have learned to actively minister in public. I'm an introvert who processes the hustle and bustle of the world in solitude and silence. But my ministry has also forced me to get along with a lot of people. I am outgoing in a crowd. I like to get along with folks and find it easy to do so. I was a conscientious objector in the Vietnam War, and was ready to die for my beliefs in peace, although I respect those who differ with me. I like to think of myself as a peaceful man. Still, I can become upset when my neat little world of inner peace is upset. I like closure, neatness. I like things to make sense.

It's easy to be peaceful when all is going well. We can usually even stay peaceful when facing the rather normal ups and downs in life. It is far more difficult when we face big challenges. It's also true when little things pile up, one upon the other, when nothing seems to go right with our day, or even with our life! This is what St. Francis is addressing here.

Jesus says,

> You have heard that it was said, "You shall love your neighbor and hate your enemy." But I say to you, Love your enemies and pray for those who persecute you, so that you may be sons of your Father who is in heaven; for he makes his sun rise on the evil and on the good, and sends rain on the just and on the unjust. For if you love those who love you, what reward have you? Do not even the tax collectors do the same? And if you salute only your brethren, what more are you doing than others? Do not even the Gentiles do the same? You, therefore, must be perfect, as your heavenly Father is perfect. (Matt. 5:43–48)

And St. Paul says,

> Repay no one evil for evil, but take thought for what is noble in the sight of all. If possible, so far as it depends upon you, live peaceably with all. Beloved, never avenge yourselves, but leave it to the wrath of God; for it is written, "Vengeance is mine, I will repay, says the Lord." No, "if your enemy is hungry, feed him; if he is thirsty, give him drink; for by so doing you will heap burning coals upon his head." Do not be overcome by evil, but overcome evil with good. (Rom. 12:18–21)

So peace is not just an external peace, when all is going well. Peace is something deeper, something more lasting and abiding than the unavoidable and often upsetting ups and downs of life. How do we obtain this peace? First, it is a gift. Jesus says, "But the Counselor, the Holy Spirit, whom the

Father will send in my name, he will teach you all things, and bring to your remembrance all that I have said to you. Peace I leave with you; my peace I give to you; not as the world gives do I give to you. Let not your hearts be troubled, neither let them be afraid" (John 14:26–27). This is not a worldly peace. The military or the civil police cannot bring it. Politics cannot bring it. Culture and social justice cannot bring it. Only Jesus can bring it fully. But how? What actually happens to us that brings this peace? Jesus says that it is the Holy Spirit, who brings his words to our heart.

How do we receive the Holy Spirit? Sure, we receive the Spirit through baptism, and especially confirmation in the West, or chrismation in the East. We also receive it through the Word of God, and interaction with our Christian family and community. But how does this happen from our end? What can we do to facilitate this? You must ask! "If you then, who are evil, know how to give good gifts to your children, how much more will the heavenly Father give the Holy Spirit to those who ask him!" (Lk. 11:13).

St. Paul teaches his spiritual son St. Timothy, "I remind you to rekindle the gift of God that is within you through the laying on of my hands; for God did not give us a spirit of timidity but a spirit of power and love and self-control" (2 Tim. 1:6–7). The Greek for "rekindle" means to "stir up," "inflame," or "fan into flame." It requires some action to facilitate the gift of the Holy Spirit in our life. We are always "indwelt" by the Spirit (Rom. 8:9), but we must also be "filled" with the Spirit (Eph. 5:18). This, too, is a gift (Acts 2:38).

I am reminded of an illustration my spiritual father once showed me. He handed me his Bible. He held it out as a complete gift. He told me not to reach out and receive it. Obviously, I couldn't receive the gift. No matter how many times he held his Bible out to me, I couldn't receive it if I didn't reach back and receive it into my own hands. The same is true with the gift of the Holy Spirit. We must learn how to cooperate with grace to fully activate it in our life. Yes, the gift is given, and that affects our response to reach back to receive. But if we do not actually follow up on that effect of grace in our life, no matter how really God offers his Holy Spirit, it will not be activated in our life on a practical level.

In the Catholic Charismatic Renewal we used to tell people who wanted the gift of tongues or singing in the Spirit that it would never happen if they weren't willing to open their mouths and make a sound. Some folks feel that such expressions are somehow beneath them, or too childish. We aren't to be childish, but unless we are willing to become like little children again, we cannot really know the maturity that is ours in Christ. It is similar with the fruit of the Spirit. St. Paul tells us that the fruit is activated through the cross (Gal. 5:24–25). It is only when the old, falsely sophisticated self dies that we can be born again a completely new person in the real wisdom of Christ.

This reminds me of the story of St. Francis and one of the disobedient brothers. I will paraphrase a rather humorous version that my spiritual father passed on to me. There was a disobedient brother who remained disobedient no matter how hard both he and the brothers tried to cure him. So Francis ordered that a hole be dug behind the friary. He buried that brother in it up to his neck! He left him there for a few hours. He asked him, "Are you dead yet?" The brother said no. So Francis left him there. This went on a few times. At one point the brother said, "I'm just angry that you left me in this hole!" Finally, after a day or so, Francis came back and asked again, "Are you dead yet?" The brother responded, "Yes, I am dead now." He had finally let go of his old resistance to letting the old self die in Christ. No harm had come to the brother. In fact, he was born again.

While such a practice would be condemned as extreme, even abusive, today, it remains a good illustration of how we must let the old self die and be buried in Christ, so that we might also be resurrected and born again in him. The old self must die before we can have lasting peace. When the old self is dead there is no one to get angry when things don't go our way, or when we face obstacles or opposition. All that is left is Jesus. St. Paul speaks of this in his own life when he says, "I have been crucified with Christ; it is no longer I who live, but Christ who lives in me" (Gal. 2:20).

St. Francis says to imagine a dead body. It offers no resistance to being moved. If you move its hands, it does not resist. It no longer cares. The more it is honored with colorful garments, the paler it looks. It no longer cares about worldly honors or shame. Once more, this might be an extreme example, but it graphically illustrates the point: If you have died to your old self in Christ, you have interior peace no matter what happens to you in this world.

Once we have this inner peace, we have something to really share with the world. You cannot give what you do not have, and you cannot give away something you do not possess. You cannot evangelize until you have been evangelized, and you cannot bring real peace if you do not experience peace in your heart. But once you discover it, you must share it with everyone you meet. Then our evangelization, and peace and justice of programs begin to really work, for we carry a peace that passes all understanding!

St. Paul concludes: "Rejoice in the Lord always; again I will say, Rejoice. Let all men know your forbearance. The Lord is at hand. Have no anxiety about anything, but in everything by prayer and supplication with thanksgiving let your requests be made known to God. And the peace of God, which passes all understanding, will keep your hearts and your minds in Christ Jesus" (Phil. 4:4–7). This is the peace that Francis of Assisi experienced, and shared with others.

Admonition 16
Purity of Heart

⌇⌇⌒⌐⊙ ST. FRANCIS WROTE:

"Blessed are the clean of heart, for they shall see God"
(Matt. 5:8). A person is truly clean of heart when they
have no time for the things of this world, but is continually
searching for the things of heaven, never failing to keep
God before their eyes, always adoring him with a heart
and soul that are pure.

The Greek word for clean means "pure." It is used of
pruning vines of fruitless growth, and of ritual and
moral purity. It is used in Jesus's upbraiding of the
religious leaders of his day, who cleansed the outside through
scrupulous ritual purity, while remaining impure within. Jesus
says clearly, "Woe to you, scribes and Pharisees, hypocrites! for
you cleanse the outside of the cup and of the plate, but inside
they are full of extortion and rapacity. You blind Pharisee! first
cleanse the inside of the cup and of the plate, that the outside
also may be clean" (Matt. 23:25–26). The Greek for *hypocrite*
means "actor" or "pretender."

It is not enough to get the rituals and rubrics right to please
God. They only point to the reason for their existence: to
bring us into a personal encounter with God through Jesus,

in the power of the Holy Spirit. You can fold your hands just right, kneel at all the right times, and still be far from God. You can even get your theology and ecclesiology right, and still be wrong in your relationship with God.

The notion of pruning is also important, though less obvious in English. Pruning trims back unfruitful growth. Some of it is obvious. Some branches are dead and dry. Others are alive and green, but they bear no fruit. They must be pruned away so more life will be sent to the ones that are fruitful. This is less obvious. We trim off otherwise live branches that will never bear fruit. This is "cleaning" a vine. Jesus says, "I am the true vine, and my Father is the vinedresser. Every branch of mine that bears no fruit, he takes away, and every branch that does bear fruit he prunes, that it may bear more fruit. You are already made clean by the word which I have spoken to you" (John 15:1–3). This purity, or cleanness of heart, is achieved by pruning our lives of things that are evil, or even of things that might be otherwise good but are unfruitful. What we are interiorly is made known externally by the fruit of our life. And we bear the fruit of the Spirit.

Pruning is sometimes pleasing and comfortable, and sometimes downright painful. When we trim off dead branches it doesn't hurt; it clears room for living branches to spread and grow; it allows us to breathe. But it is painful when we trim branches that are alive but not fruitful. Likewise, sometimes the pruning process feels good, like getting a good massage or back alignment. At other times, it is initially painful and unpleasant. The things that are unfruitful have sometimes taken over and are deeply ingrained in our behavior. To prune and remove them causes pain in the short term. But in the long term it brings us more life and fruit.

I remember when a big mulberry tree next to a farmhouse where I lived in Indiana was pruned. I loved that tree. It was huge, and it provided lovely shade for the house in the hot summers. But its limbs were off balance and threatening the roof of the house. So we decided to have it trimmed. We called the tree service, and they came out in a few days. I went to work in the fields the day they came. I expected to come back to a tree with the dangerous branches neatly trimmed, but still large and lovely. Boy, was I surprised! I came back to a trunk with a few little green sprigs at the top. I was devastated. I thought they had killed my lovely tree. But I was wrong. The next year it came back strong, and the year after was bigger than ever, but balanced and safe. In fact, I put a wonderful tire swing on it where I spent many a late afternoon swinging and contemplating the wonder of God in the trees and the clouds above.

I also grew a two-acre organic garden when I was young. I pruned a lot of plants and fruit trees. I remember pruning the tomato plants, for instance. There are sucker branches that grow up between every two fruitful ones. It's easy to just pinch them off when they are just starting to appear, but much more difficult when they take hold and grow into branches equal in size to the fruitful ones. They are green, fully alive, and even beautiful in the overall appearance of the tomato plant. But they suck life from the fruitful branches. They must be pruned to have a truly fruitful tomato plant. So when we let God prune us, he brings back balance and fruitfulness, and provides a great environment for praise and contemplation.

This Admonition relates pruning to something quite specific: worldliness. We are to be in the world but not of the world. We are not to be worldly. In common English, *worldly* originally meant something more positive than it does today. It meant being experienced, sophisticated, wise, or well-traveled. These are things that can be positive, even desirable. Biblical worldliness is another thing. The Greek word used in Scripture for "world" is *kosmos* and means everything from the orderly and harmonious arrangement of the earth and the entire universe, including humanity, to humanity fallen away from God. But it is largely positive. The word for worldly also translates as "flesh" or "carnal." It is clearly negative.

In the negative, St. Paul contrasts the Spirit and the world when he says,

> Has not God made foolish the wisdom of the world? For since, in the wisdom of God, the world did not know God through wisdom, it pleased God through the folly of what we preach to save those who believe. For Jews demand signs and Greeks seek wisdom, but we preach Christ crucified, a stumbling block to Jews and folly to Gentiles, but to those who are called, both Jews and Greeks, Christ the power of God and the wisdom of God. For the foolishness of God is wiser than men, and the weakness of God is stronger than men. (1 Cor. 1:20–25)

He goes on to affirm that worldly wisdom or training is not necessary for a follower of Jesus. "For consider your call, brethren; not many of you were wise according to worldly standards, not many were powerful, not many were of noble birth; but God chose what is foolish in the world to shame the wise, God chose what is weak in the world to shame the strong" (1 Cor. 1:26–27).

What exactly is this negative worldliness? St. John tells us: "Do not love the world or the things in the world. If any one loves the world, love for the Father is not in him. For all that is in the world, the lust of the flesh and the lust of the eyes and the pride of life, is not of the Father but is of the world. And the world passes away, and the lust of it; but he who does the will of God abides for ever" (1 John 2:15–17). This is similar to "carnality," or the negative use of the word "passions," by the early monastic fathers and mothers.

In this Admonition, St. Francis says, "A person is really clean of heart when they have no time for the things of this world, but are continually searching for the things of heaven, never failing to keep God before their eyes, and always adoring him with a heart and soul that are pure." This is radical! He is saying that we combat worldliness, passion, and desire by always keeping the Lord before our eyes, and adoring him. On one level, cleansing our soul prepares us for proper worship. On another, the very act of worshiping and adoring cleanses the soul and prepares it for more of God. So when we worship God authentically, the acts of adoration, worship, and praise defeat the negative aspects of worldliness, passions, and desires.

It is like water and oil. Water always displaces oil. If you fill your soul with the positive things of God through worship and praise you almost naturally displace the things that aren't of God. You simply won't have room or time in your life for the negative. We enter the presence of the Lord two ways, through repentance, and through praise and thanks. After these we are more open to word and sacrament.

Repentance means changing your mind. The biblical word is *metanoia*. It comes from *meta*, which means "with," and *nous*, which means "mind." It is foundational to the Gospel. In fact, Jesus's first sermon was, "Repent, for the kingdom of heaven is at hand" (Matt. 4:17). Jesus calls us to change, and change for the better! We do that simply by making up our mind to do it, and to let go of old ways so we might fully embrace the way, truth, and life of Jesus with the assistance of the Holy Spirit. There is no sin that we cannot turn from, and no one is turned away from God's grace if we really seek him.

But we also enter God's presence and stir up the Spirit in our life through thanksgiving and praise. "Enter his gates with thanksgiving, and his courts with praise" (Ps. 100:4). And, "Let us come into his presence with thanksgiving; let us make a joyful noise to him with songs of praise!" (Ps. 95:2). St. Paul tells us to thank God always and for everything (Eph. 5:20). This means intentionally taking time to find the good in every day. It is there if we really take time to look. It also means that we thank God for the seemingly bad things, for even these things unite us with the cross and have lessons to teach when approached with faith (Rom. 8:28). Such an attitude of gratitude truly cleans our minds and hearts of negativity that leads to sin and walking death.

St. Francis invites us to really have clean hearts. He invites us to turn from negative worldliness, passions, and desires. He invites us to really enter God's presence through adoration, worship, thanks, and praise. If we respond to his invitation, our lives will be transformed.

Admonition 17
The Humble Religious

ST. FRANCIS WROTE:

"Blessed is that servant" (Matt. 24:46) who takes no more pride in the good that God says and does through them, than in that which God says and does through someone else. It is wrong for anyone to be anxious to receive more from his neighbor than he himself is willing to give to God.

This really gets down to it—again! Most of us have a hard time seeing this as possible, much less desirable. Pride runs strong in most of us, and it hides under religious clothing. St. Francis is taking us to a spirituality that is head and shoulders above the way most of us operate in our Christian lives. If we will dare to listen to his teaching, absorb it without typical arguments, and let it soak into our souls, we might find a whole new way of freedom that was, and is, the way of the saints.

The substance of this Admonition, like many of the others, is humility. Francis says elsewhere that humility is the truth. He says, "What a person is before God, that he is, and nothing more."

The English word *humility* comes from the Latin, meaning humus, or earth and ground. The primary Greek word for humility is *tapeino*. It means to be abased or brought low. Some say it means to be brought to the earth. Jesus says, "He who is greatest among you shall be your servant; whoever exalts himself will be humbled, and whoever humbles himself will be exalted" (Matt. 23:11–12). He also says, "Whoever humbles himself like this child, he is the greatest in the kingdom of heaven" (Matt. 18:4).

I am reminded of the story of Blessed Giles of Assisi, one of St. Francis's first followers. There was an early leader named Brother Elias. He was educated and most apt regarding the administration of the new community. He succeeded St. Francis to leadership and was even used by the church for diplomatic missions to estranged civil rulers and nations. But the brothers didn't like Elias's. They saw him as haughty and self-serving. Many irregularities arose in his life of gospel poverty and resulted in his abuse of power. The brothers asked for church intervention, and it ended with Brother Elias's being deposed from leadership. But he was still used by the church for diplomacy. At one point, he found himself caught crossways in the timing between his diplomatic mission to the emperor and the pope excommunicating that same emperor. He incurred a de facto excommunication. But instead of quickly coming clean through a simple act of humility and confession, he found himself briefly outside of the graces of the church. When Brother Giles heard of Elias's excommunication by the church he immediately fell to the ground and groveled in the dust and dirt. When asked why he did this, he said, "I want to get as low to the ground as possible, so that if I also fall I won't have far to go!" He understood that humility is being brought low to the earth.

Another word for humility is *praus*, which means meek, mild, or gentle. Jesus used this word when he preached the Sermon on the Mount. He says, "Blessed are the meek [*praus*], for they shall inherit the earth" (Matt. 5:5).[2] He also uses it in,

2 Catholic Biblical Association (Great Britain) (1994).

"Tell the daughter of Zion, Behold, your king is coming to you, humble [*praus*], and mounted on an ass, and on a colt, the foal of an ass" (Matt. 21:5).

And Jesus is the primary example of this for us.

How do we get this humility? St. Paul tells us that it is, as with so many virtues, a fruit of the Spirit in our life: "But the fruit of the Spirit is love, joy, peace, patience, kindness, goodness, faithfulness, gentleness, self-control; against such there is no law" (Gal. 5:22–23). We must learn to stir up the Spirit. Those who are baptized and confirmed already have the Spirit. He dwells within us. But there is a difference between simply being indwelt by the Spirit and filled with the Spirit. We must learn how to stir up the Spirit through praise and thanks, repentance, and a changed way of life. Then we can be filled with the Spirit, not only in exceptional moments, but also as a regular and even a daily experience.

St. Francis gives us a higher challenge. We are to take pride not when we are praised, but when others are. This is easy with close family and friends, but it's difficult in ordinary situations with people we aren't close to, or who we might not like. This seems almost impossible, at least by human standards, but it is tied in with a true body-of-Christ spirituality in the church. If one member is praised, we all are (1 Cor. 12:26). If humility is the truth, the truth is this: We are incomplete without one another in Christ. Each has a natural and supernatural gift that the other does not possess, or at least not in the same way the other does. In this I can see something in every other person in humanity, and specifically in the church and the monastic community, that I don't have. They use this gift better than I do (Phil. 2:3). Conversely, I have a gift that they do not have. But if we understand that all belong to Jesus, I do not get proud, or envious and resentful. This is good news!

The Rule of St. Benedict elaborates something similar in chapter 7, "On Humility." St. Benedict says, "The seventh step of humility is that a man not only admits with his tongue but is also convinced in his heart that he is inferior to all and of less value, humbling himself." If it were not for a correct understanding of humility and the spirituality of the body of Christ in the church and the monastic community, this would be downright masochistic. As it is, it is something truly beautiful. It requires that we bring the old insecure, self-obsessed, envious, jealous, and resentful self to the cross, and let it go. Only then can we be raised up as new persons in the resurrection of Jesus Christ and become the persons God created us to be.

This is a process, and that's why Benedict included step seven as only one in twelve steps of humility. The steps are these:

1. That we keep the presence of God before us always, and be in awe of God.
2. That we renounce our old self will.
3. That this be incarnated and tested by submitting to a valid leader.
4. That we remain humbly obedient even in difficult situations.
5. That we reveal our thoughts to our spiritual leaders so that they can help us in our spiritual journey in Christ.
6. That we are satisfied with the lowliest tasks, as well as the great ones.
7. That we consider others as superior to ourselves.
8. That we only do what is the common work according to the rule of the monastery.
9. That we control our tongues and keep silent whenever possible.
10 That we not be given to false laughter that exalts the ego.
11 That when we speak we do so humbly and gently.
12. That humility transforms our entire life.

These steps are radical and countercultural. It is true, they can be applied superficially and become really weird—but when they are applied in the context of letting go of the old self and rising as a new creation in Christ they make a lot of sense. They also bring great freedom and joy.

At Little Portion Hermitage and Monastery, we invoke the patronage of both Franciscan and Benedictine saints. Specifically, we invoke "St. Francis and St. Clare, St. Benedict and St. Scholastica." We find that, while they emphasize different aspects of gospel living of consecration, they complement and complete one another.

Are we humble or proud? Are we rooted in the truth or in illusion about ourselves, others, and creation? Do we find ourselves completed or obstructed when working with others? These are telling questions about how well we have learned the lesson of this Admonition.

Admonition 18
Compassion for One's Neighbor

꒰꒱ ST. FRANCIS WROTE:

Blessed are servants of God who are patient with their neighbors' shortcomings in the way that they would like those neighbors to support them, if the situation were reversed. Blessed also are the ones who thank God for all that is good, because whoever keeps something for themselves, it is as if they "dug in the ground and hid his master's money" (Matt. 25:18), and what they thought they had "will be taken away" (Lk. 8:18).

Shortcomings and sins mean to fall short of God or others. The main biblical word for sin is *hamartia*, which refers to getting off the path. We might want to go the right direction, but we fall off the path and become lost: "all have sinned and fall short of the glory of God" (Rom. 3:23). Usually this happens one step at a time, little by little, but the end result is getting lost and not arriving at our desired destination. So, sin is both less radical and more serious than we often think. Here in the Ozarks, people sometimes wander off the path in the woods and get really turned around and lost! Few intend it; they want to go the right direction, but because they didn't follow directions they end up lost and confused.

Loving God and loving your neighbor as yourself is the foundation of all the moral teaching of Jesus. He says, "You shall love the Lord your God with all your heart, and with all your soul, and with all your mind. This is the great and first commandment. And a second is like it, You shall love your neighbor as yourself. On these two commandments depend all the law and the prophets" (Matt. 22:37–40). Some have modernized this to mean that we must first love ourselves before we can love others. While this jells with modern psychology, and it certainly makes some sense, it is probably not what Jesus meant. This teaching of Jesus assumes that we already love ourselves, and love ourselves a bit too much! He emphasizes that we must get our focus off ourselves and onto God and others. Then we will discover a whole new way of living, get free of self-preoccupation, and find real freedom. As he says, whoever loses their life for his sake will really find it (Matt. 10:19).

Jesus also says in the Sermon on the Mount, "So whatever you wish that men would do to you, do so to them" (Matt. 7:12). This is the famous Golden Rule found in Christian scripture, and in other religions. "Do not do to others what you would not like yourself" says the Confucian *Analects*. In the Talmud of Judaism: "What is hateful to you, do not do to your fellowman. This is the entire Law; all the rest is commentary." There are similar examples from most major religions of the world. It also applies to forgiveness of others' shortcomings. St. Paul says, "As the Lord has forgiven you, so you also must forgive" (Col. 3:13).

We love to judge. We especially love to judge other people. We tend to be forgiving with ourselves, but judgmental with others. Some have said that our culture is being choked with the "blame game." We do this with politicians and church leaders. We live rather free lives regarding sin, but we expect them to live up to standards that we ourselves seldom embrace. Ironically, this often stems from self-hatred and a low self-identity. Because we are not sure of ourselves, we project that need for perfection onto others—but they can never satisfy the need we really have within ourselves, so we end up judging them harshly, while we continue stuck in our old patterns. This is an emotional death cycle, and Jesus shows us a way out. We have already addressed having a healthy understanding of creation and redemption in Jesus.

This Admonition addresses patience with other people's shortcomings. It implies forgiveness as well. It is one thing to turn back from sin. It is another thing to be received by the people still on the path—to be forgiven, both by God and by his people. We hear all throughout Scripture that God forgives those who sincerely and honestly turn back to him with a humble and contrite heart. But it's hard for God's people to forgive the ones who have left them.

In the early church, St. Cyprian of Carthage wrote a groundbreaking book, *On the Lapsed*. The debate he was undertaking was about those who had apostatized, meaning that they had turned from faith in Jesus to save their own life and limb under persecution. When the persecution was over they came back to the church and wanted to be forgiven and received back as if nothing had happened. But for the ones who had lost husbands, wives, family members, beloved brothers and sisters in Christ, or perhaps a limb or an eye, while staying faithful to the faith, it was not so easy. Were they supposed to just forgive and say, "Come on back"? The rigorists maintained that if they sinned after accepting Christ, there was no more forgiveness for them (see Heb. 6:4–6). Wasn't this the unforgiveable sin (see Matt. 12:31)?

But Cyprian maintained that forgiveness is available to all after a period of penance to test the quality of their repentance (see Matt. 3:8). They confessed their sin before the bishop, who assigned them a period of penance. Sometimes they had to remain penitents for a long time, even years, fellowshipping with the church, but without receiving Communion. If they were serious they would persevere. If not, they would get angry and leave. For those who persevered, the bishop would declare them forgiven in public before the congregation so the matter would be over, with no room for condemnation or gossip. This became the pattern of the developing early church.

St. Benedict has a provision to receive those who left the community back into fellowship if it worked out. But he didn't require this of all communities in every case. It was based on discernment by the community and the leaders, especially the abbot. He says, "If a brother, following his own evil ways, leaves the monastery but then wishes to return, he must first promise to make full amends for leaving. Let him be received back, but as a test of his humility he should be given the last place. If he leaves again, or even a third time, he should be readmitted under the same conditions. After this, however, he must understand that he will be denied all prospect of return (RB 23).

There are a couple of words for "forgive" and "forgiveness" in the New Testament. The first and most used is *aphiemi*. It means "to leave, forgive, suffer, let, forsake, let alone." I have heard it taught that it could mean to send away, as in divorcing a spouse. So this means to send away the sins of others and forsake them like a person who divorces their spouse. We put them totally behind us. The other word is *charizomai*. It is interesting that one of the roots of this form is *charis*, which means "grace" or "gift." This is at the root of *charisma, charismatic,* and even is seen in *Eucharist*. Eucharist, *eucharistia*, is usually translated "thanksgiving." But the roots are *eu*, "good," and *charizomai*, or "forgiveness." It is a "good forgiveness, a thanksgiving." It is interesting that joy, or *chara*, is also similar to *charis*, and *charizomai.* When we forgive, we create joy. When we withhold forgiveness, we bring sorrow. This power is given to all Christians. When we forgive, we loose the power of heaven in ourselves, and in those we forgive. We also bind the evil of negativity, self-hatred, and unnecessary guilt. We spread love, joy, and peace. When we withhold forgiveness we bind up other people and ourselves; we inhibit the full working of the Holy Spirit in our lives.

Miracles are unleashed in our life when we have faith that moves mountains, and when we forgive. Jesus teaches: "Have faith in God. Truly, I say to you, whoever says to this mountain, 'Be taken up and cast into the sea,' and does not doubt in his heart, but believes that what he says will come to pass, it will be done for him. Therefore I tell you, whatever you ask in prayer, believe that you receive it, and you will. And whenever you stand praying, forgive, if you have anything against any one; so that your Father also who is in heaven may forgive you your trespasses" (Mk. 11:22–25). So we are to have faith that personifies in the now what we hope for the future, but also forgiving "anything against anyone." This is part of what it means to be transformed in Christ.

St. Francis taught the leaders of his community that there is no brother in the whole world, no matter how far he has fallen into sin, who could not be called back to forgiveness simply by looking into your eyes. This is radical. You cannot hide your disdain or judgment of others. It is seen in your eyes, which are the windows of the soul. If you forgive and really love, it will shine through your eyes. As a Cajun nun once asked me, "Is Jesus in your heart?" I said with determination, "Yes!" She said, "Then, please inform your face!" The face and the eyes put on full display whatever is in your heart and soul.

But this Admonition is not merely about forgiveness. It is also about patience with those who sin. God is patient with us— and we are to be patient and forgiving in response! Sirach says,

"Await God's patience, cling to him and do not depart, that you may be wise in all your ways. Accept whatever is brought upon you, and endure it in sorrow; in changes that humble you be patient" (Sir. 2:3–4).

In Matthew 18, Jesus, teaching on patience and forgiveness, tells the story of the unjust steward. The steward asks, and obtains forgiveness: "So the servant fell on his knees, imploring him, 'Lord, have patience with me, and I will pay you everything.' And out of pity for him the lord of that servant released him and forgave him the debt." But he would not offer similar forgiveness to those who asked the same thing of him. "But that same servant, as he went out, came upon one of his fellow servants who owed him a hundred denarii; and seizing him by the throat he said, 'Pay what you owe.' So his fellow servant fell down and besought him, '*Have patience with me,* and I will pay you.' He refused and went and put him in prison till he should pay the debt." This did not go well for the unjust steward. "Then his lord summoned him and said to him, 'You wicked servant! I forgave you all that debt because you besought me; and should not you have had mercy on your fellow servant, as I had mercy on you?' And in anger his lord delivered him to the jailers, till he should pay all his debt." As St. Paul said, must forgive as we've been forgiven (Col.2:13).

The primary moral of this Admonition? We must be patient with sinners and forgive them with sincerity. "So also my heavenly Father will do to every one of you, if you do not forgive your brother from your heart" (Matt. 18:35). By nature, most of us are impatient. I know I am! But I pray, "Lord, give me patience, and I want it now!" How can we become patient?

St. Paul says that he is patient because Jesus was patient with him. When we meditate on this we are humbled, and our old nature is calmed. He says, "And I am the foremost of sinners; but I received mercy for this reason, that in me, as the foremost, Jesus Christ might display his perfect patience for an example to those who were to believe in him for eternal life" (1 Tim. 1:15–16). But sometimes even this is not enough. It remains a human response to a divine gift, but it still falls short of anything organic and lasting in the core of our being. In Galatians 5:23, Paul lists patience among the fruit of the Spirit. The Spirit brings the very person of Jesus within us. This means it cannot be had without the grace of the Holy Spirit actively empowering us.

So even when you think you cannot be patient with God, yourself, or others, do not give up! Jesus is the way, the truth, and the life. He comes to save us and give us abundant life beginning right here on earth and continuing into eternal life. When the old impatient and judgmental self dies with Christ on the cross, then a new person of patience, inner peace, and forgiveness rises through the resurrection of Jesus. That's good news!

Admonition 19

The Virtuous and Humble Servant of God

꙳ ST. FRANCIS WROTE:

Blessed are the servants of God who have no more regard
for themselves when people praise them and make much
of them than when they despise and criticize them and say
that they are ignorant. What a person is before God, so
they are and no more. Beware servants of God, if you have
been put in a position of authority by others, if you are not
anxious to leave it behind. On the other hand, blessed are
the servants of God who are placed high against their will,
and still want to be counted lower than others.

This Admonition is about confidence and authority.
The English words *authority* and *author* are related.
Real authority is in knowing the authorship of Christ
in our personal life. Once we know that authority, we are happy
whether or not we are in leadership, in positions of authority,
or "lower than others."

I am reminded of the legend of St. Bonaventure, a follower of
St. Francis, and a leader of the Franciscan order. Bonaventure
received his cardinal's hat while washing dishes in a hermitage.

Instead of interrupting his household duties in the hermitage, he had those who brought the hat from the pope hang it on the branches of the tree outside the hermitage! Bonaventure understood real authority because he was confident of his place and authority in Christ (Heb. 4:16; 1 Pet. 1:21).

St. Paul says, "But far be it from me to glory except in the cross of our Lord Jesus Christ, by which the world has been crucified to me, and I to the world" (Gal. 6:14). This confidence transforms our worldly defeats into victories. Indeed, we are told to actively embrace the cross of Christ, and to seek it. This gives us complete freedom from the emotional swings of triumphs and tragedies, joys and sorrows. It brings us love, joy, and peace amid the inevitable ups and downs of this earthly life, even in the church.

Francis also mentions criticism. How well do we handle criticism? In public ministry, a person cannot escape it. I've had people actually threaten to shoot me, even in a church! I've been protested by Protestants who disagreed with my conversion to Catholicism, and I've been shuffled out of concerts by police in the Middle East when my simple gospel message didn't line up with Christian, Muslim, and Jewish extremists. More personally, I've had people criticize my leadership in community. Some of this was trivial, and some of it was serious. The serious and mean-spirited accusations were always hurtful, especially when they came from people I truly loved and was trying to help. Though I tried to rise above it and walk with charity even with my accusers, it certainly wasn't easy, and required walking by faith and not by sight. St. Paul certainly had to rise above the criticisms of those he called false apostles (2 Cor. 2:13) and false brothers (Gal. 2:4). So, I am not alone.

The closest thing in Scripture to this is the notion of persecution and being "reviled." Of course, Jesus says, "Blessed are those who are persecuted for righteousness' sake, for theirs is the kingdom of heaven. Blessed are you when men revile you and persecute you and utter all kinds of evil against you falsely on my account. Rejoice and be glad, for your reward is great in heaven, for so men persecuted the prophets who were before you." (Matt. 5:10–12). The Greek for "revile" means to upbraid or to "cast in one's teeth." This violent language is used to emphasize the emotional impact of harsh criticism. We cannot ignore the emotional impact with which it is given, nor the normal reaction our old self would have without grace. But we can respond now with love, joy, and peace in Christ.

So this is when he says to rejoice? Yes! We should calmly consider criticism in case it is just. If just, we should repent and humbly ask forgiveness and change. If unjust, we can rejoice insofar as it enables us to share in the sufferings of Christ. Either way, it causes us to respond, not with resistance, but with love for the one criticizing us. Jesus teaches,

> You have heard that it was said, "You shall love your neighbor and hate your enemy." But I say to you, Love your enemies and pray for those who persecute you, so that you may be sons of your Father who is in heaven; for he makes his sun rise on the evil and on the good, and sends rain on the just and on the unjust. For if you love those who love you, what reward have you? Do not even the tax collectors do the same? And if you salute only your brethren, what more are you doing than others? Do not even the Gentiles do the same? You, therefore, must be perfect, as your heavenly Father is perfect.
> (Matt. 5:43–48)

This is a high calling. No political party or earthly nation espouses it fully. Few religions practice it. Only Jesus brings it.

But Jesus is also realistic. He gives a plan for how to escape at least some of it. He says that when we encounter such resistance and ill treatment, if we are able, we simply move on to another place. He says,

> Brother will deliver up brother to death, and the father his child, and children will rise against parents and have them put to death; and you will be hated by all for my name's sake. But he who endures to the end will be saved. When they persecute you in one town, flee to the next; for truly, I say to you, you will not have gone through all the towns of Israel, before the Son of man comes.
>
> A disciple is not above his teacher, nor a servant above his master; it is enough for the disciple to be like his teacher, and the servant like his master. If they have called the master of the house Beelzebul, how much more will they malign those of his household. So have no fear of them. (Matt. 10:21–26)

In Luke's Gospel Jesus even says to "shake off the dust" from your feet as you move on (Lk. 9:5). He does not mean that this should be done in anger. We are still to love our enemy from the heart. It is simply a matter of not forcing the gospel of Jesus down anyone's throat. If they are not ready to receive it, simply move on. But this isn't always soft and fluffy. It has some teeth for those who do not respond well when criticized. Of those who turn from Jesus in the face of such persecution, he warns, "As for what was sown on rocky ground, this is he who hears the word and immediately receives it with joy; yet he has no root in himself, but endures for a while, and when tribulation or persecution arises on account of the word, immediately he falls away" (Matt. 13:20–21).

He also says to literally flee to the mountains and wilderness when we are persecuted: "Let those who are in Judea flee to the mountains; let him who is on the housetop not go down to take what is in his house; and let him who is in the field not turn back to take his mantle. And alas for those who are with child and for those who give suck in those days! Pray that your flight may not be in winter or on a Sabbath" (Matt. 24:16–20). One account says that the first Christian hermit, St. Paul of the Desert, went to the desert when his family persecuted him, and threatened to turn him in for being a Christian. Later generations would go to the desert by choice.

Scripture also talks about not engaging in negative speech in the face of such wrongful treatment. St. Paul summarizes, "For I fear that perhaps I may come and find you not what I wish, and that you may find me not what you wish; that perhaps there may be quarreling, jealousy, anger, selfishness, slander, gossip, conceit, and disorder" (2 Cor. 12:20). Suffice it to say that gossip is saying something that might be right but is spoken to the wrong person; slander is saying something false. Unfortunately, what begins as gossip often morphs into slander by the time the tale is told a few times to the wrong people. We are not to complain about, gossip about, or slander those who persecute us. We are to genuinely bless them from our heart.

St. Francis once again reminds leaders that they should be anxious to step away from leadership as soon as asked to do so by their community or higher legitimate authority. I am reminded of how Francis himself resigned the leadership of the very order and movement he founded. It is no secret that Francis was not a great organizer, though his dream of an international mendicant order with one leader was something new for his era. It is also no secret that the idealism of Francis caused his brothers no small discomfort. They were uncomfortable with his rugged and no-nonsense gospel simplicity. Ironically, they didn't want to embrace the poverty he preached, which is what had initially attracted them. They wanted him to write a Rule for himself, but not for them. Brother Elias even "lost" the Rule Francis wrote so as to not have to obey it! It is said that the stigmata were an external sign of the anguish Francis felt in his heart after seeing the order he founded stray so far from his teaching. Francis's resignation was his way of simply letting go and letting God.

I have seen this humility in many leaders who come to the end of their leadership term, and humbly return to the status as a simple member, though we honor them for their service, and new leaders seek their advice. Such an example blesses me more than they will ever know. I also sadly sometimes see the contrary. Sometimes, when a person grows accustomed to leadership, they begin to attach their self-identity to the role, and find it nearly impossible to let it go. This is always tragic.

Whether one is thrust into leadership or feels comfortable there, St. Francis tells us to fully embrace the cross of Jesus Christ. We must let go of our ego attachments that create a false self-identity with work or position, and die with Christ. Then, and only then, can we rise up a new creation in the resurrection of Jesus, and become the person God originally created us to be.

Is our confidence solely in Christ? Is it rooted in humility or pride? How well do we handle, not only praise, but also criticism? How well do we handle losing our position in the church, our community, or the secular world? These are lessons from St. Francis, not only for those are vowed religious, but for every Christian at every stage of life.

Admonition 20

The Happy and Silly
Servant of God

~∽⊙ ST. FRANCIS WROTE:

Blessed are those servants of God who find all their joy
and happiness in the words and deeds of our Lord and
use them to cause other people to love God gladly. And
beware those servants of God who spend time amusing
themselves with silly words and meaningless laughter,
leading people astray.

We live in an unhappy, angry world. Discontent is
rampant. Anger is overflowing. Politics is filled
with indignation. The tensions between residents
and immigrants are as bad as they were centuries ago. Some
say that racial tensions are worse than they were in the 1960s—
though I lived through them in the 60s, and they seem subtler
now. The "piecemeal World War III," as Pope Francis calls it,
between extremist Islam and the West makes both sides hostile.
Our culture is at a boiling point, and it is boiling over all over
the place.

We often use humor to mask these emotions. It's a
superficial mask at best. Sure, it lets off a bit of the simmering

steam, but it keeps us relating with others on a deeper level, and it remains shallow. It is also not unusual to use sarcasm to put other people or groups down without criticizing them directly. Sometimes it makes us feel more secure about our own tenuous positions to put others down with a joke. Is "laughter good for the soul"? Some laughter is good. I laugh heartily at times.

There is a difference between laughter and happiness and joy. The Wisdom Literature of the Jewish Scriptures says, "A man's attire and open-mouthed laughter, and a man's manner of walking, show what he is" (Sir. 19:30). It says that a fool lifts his head up in laughter, and a wise man smiles gently at most (Sir. 21:20). Then, "The talk of fools is offensive, and their laughter is wantonly sinful. The talk of men given to swearing makes one's hair stand on end, and their quarrels make a man stop his ears. The strife of the proud leads to bloodshed, and their abuse is grievous to hear" (Sir. 27:13–15). This sounds too familiar in today's world.

Continuing that wisdom tradition in early Christianity, St. James says, "Let your laughter be turned to mourning and your joy to dejection. Humble yourselves before the Lord and he will exalt you" (Jas. 4:9–10). This is because "the heart of the wise is in the house of mourning; but the heart of fools is in the house of mirth" (Eccles. 7:4). This is also why Paul says, "Rejoice with those who rejoice, weep with those who weep. Live in harmony with one another; do not be haughty, but associate with the lowly; never be conceited" (Rom. 12:15–16).

This is why Christian monastic tradition takes such a cautious view of humor. The Rule of St. Benedict says in chapter 7, "On the Steps of Humility," "The tenth step of humility is that he is not given to ready laughter, for it is written: 'Only a fool raises his voice in laughter.'" The actual quote from Sirach 21:20 is, "A fool raises his voice when he laughs, but a clever man smiles quietly." The New American Bible adds "at the most." It says, "A fool raises his voice in laughter, but the prudent man *at the most* smiles gently." In a time when "laughing Jesus" paintings are common, it might astonish some today to hear that Benedictines and Franciscans used to debate whether Jesus ever laughed. While he used subtle humor, Scripture is silent on the matter.

In this Admonition, St. Francis is concerned above all with happiness. Particularly in America, we talk a lot about the "pursuit of happiness." But what is happiness? Jesus says, "Blessed are the poor in spirit," and so on, in the Beatitudes. The Greek word *makarios* can mean "blessed" or "happy." A follower of Jesus is to be happy and filled with joy! There will be times of sorrow, but there will be a deep, abiding joy that anchors all such sadness so that it cannot overwhelm us.

I will not give all the Scriptures on joy. They are too numerous to list them all. Let me mention just a few. The biblical word *chara*, which is similar to *charis*, or gift, also forms part of the word for "forgiveness" and "Eucharist." Jesus says, "These things I have spoken to you, that my joy may be in you, and that your joy may be full" (John 15:11). St. Paul says, "But the fruit of the Spirit is love, joy, peace, patience, kindness, goodness, faithfulness, gentleness, self-control; against such there is no law" (Gal. 5:22–23). As with the entire list of the fruit of the Spirit, this is only realized in our life when we really die to our old self and rise a new person in Christ. So this is not a superficial joy. It is certainly not automatic. It is found in proportion to how we face, not only successes, but also failures in life, triumphs as well as tragedies. This joy is there through testing and trial. This joy underlies our inevitable times of sorrow. Paul also says, "May you be strengthened with all power, according to his glorious might, for all endurance and patience with joy, giving thanks to the Father, who has qualified us to share in the inheritance of the saints in light" (Col 1:11–12).

I am also reminded of St. Hilarion (291–371). He was a disciple of St. Antony the Great, brought Egyptian monasticism to Palestine, lived as a hermit who attracted thousands of followers, and then began a trek around the Mediterranean to run from the fame that followed him. So his solitary life generated a spiritual power in the Spirit that worked miracles and attracted huge crowds, which in turn encroached on his solitude, where he found his power in the first place. It is all a bit humorous! His name, Hilarion, means great joy. It is where we get the English word *hilarious*. It's clear the monastic caution against unholy laughter does not rule out even great joy!

I am an introvert by nature. I can be quite serious. In fact, as an artist I can tend to melancholy that opens deeper intuitions for me, but if left unguarded can also be a dangerous trap for negativity. Yet people also tell me I'm a funny guy. My brother tells me I was funny when I was a kid. I've always enjoyed laughing. I went through a period where that began to disappear, partly because I was growing in finding monastic silence, and partly because I wasn't very comfortable with the balance of personal holiness and leadership yet. I took myself a bit too seriously. But the older I become I am rediscovering a more childlike joy. Ultimately, I have rediscovered humor and joy simply because I no longer take myself all that seriously. I take Jesus seriously. I take salvation seriously. But I no longer consider myself very impressive. I have died with Christ, which makes me a bit more comfortable in my own skin. Therefore, I am more at ease exposing my more humorous side.

So, this Admonition focuses not so much on the dangers of superficial laughter but on deeper joy that's based on realizing all the goodness that belongs to God. All good flows from God and leads back to God. Only when we die to our superficial self that tries to find happiness independent of God can we become a new creation in God, who is fully and truly happy.

If we do not do this, even the little we think we possess will be lost. When we hang on to illusion rather than Reality, then when the illusion fades we are left with nothing. The joy of the Spirit is related directly, and perhaps proportionally, to our dying with Christ regarding our passions and desires, and our old self in general.

Admonition 21
The Talkative Religious

ST. FRANCIS WROTE:

Blessed are the servants of God who, when they speak, do not seek to gain anything, but wisely consider their words. Beware those servants of God who do not protect the good things of God "in an honest and good heart" (Lk. 8:15), and do not show them to others by what they do. Those who instead aim to show off with words "have their reward" (Matt. 6:2), and anyone hearing them will receive very little fruit.

This Admonition builds on the previous one. This one addresses holy silence and boasting.

Have you ever got into a situation where you find yourself talking just to fill empty space in a conversation? I have. I almost always feel as if I should just shut up as soon as the words have left my mouth. I have even done it in my public talks, and God help me, especially in unedited books! I sometimes feel as if I need to reach out, grab the words I just spoke, and pull them back into my mouth. But it is too late. Once spoken, they cannot be retracted, and I am left feeling the fool for it. Most of us have a problem with knowing the balance between silence and speech and knowing when to talk and when to be silent. I have gotten better at it in my later years, but in my younger years I struggled with this a lot.

We live in a world of social media. People are talking all the time, but we are communicating less and less. Our communication on social media is largely unedited, so we often spew out ideas based on emotion that we would not normally say to someone face-to-face. We use polemics rather than dialogue. Factitious extremes in the church, politics, and society have been given a voice, and a steady stream of vitriol and extreme notions sprawls across our social media newsfeeds. We can easily get upset and join the fray in a reactionary rather than a responsive way or, better yet, just let it pass. We often read and react in our posts or comments with notions from the extreme right or left that are polarizing and divisive. This is so widespread that Catholic leaders are cautioning strongly about this sin.

Something similar is true regarding the 24/7 news cycle. We watch a constant flow of mainly bad news from media sources, and they are no longer just giving us the news, but their "spin" on it. Consequently, we are filling our mind with news that is inescapably spun from the perspective of the people who hold the purse strings of a given network. It's better than a state-controlled press, but it's still far from perfect, even in the best of times. There is an old saying, "Garbage in, garbage out." Whatever we fill our mind with will eventually come out of the mouth or spill onto a page (or screen). We become what we think. If we think godly thoughts, we will be godly. If we think angry or opinionated thoughts, we will be angry and opinionated people.

St. Francis and the entire monastic and biblical tradition offer a way out. They provide an answer that can easily be applied to the modern phenomenon. Learning healthy silence with our tongue eventually sinks into the mind. From there it overflows into our whole way of living. The Franciscan and monastic discipline of healthy silence can help us silence all the noise that steals our peace.

In heaven, there is an awe-filled silence in the presence of a mystery of God. "When the Lamb opened the seventh seal, there was silence in heaven," Revelation says (8:1). Heaven is not just something waiting for us when we die. We can live more like angels here and now. The book of Sirach says, "There is one who keeps silent because he has no answer, while another keeps silent because he knows when to speak. A wise man will be silent until the right moment, but a braggart and fool goes beyond the right moment. Whoever uses too many words will be loathed, and whoever usurps the right to speak will be hated" (Sir. 20:6–10). He continues,

> Speak, young man, if there is need of you, but no more than twice, and only if asked. Speak concisely, say much in few words; be as one who knows and yet holds his tongue. Among the great do not act as their equal; and when another is speaking, do not babble. Lightning speeds before the thunder, and approval precedes a modest man. Leave in good time and do not be the last; go home quickly and do not linger. Amuse yourself there, and do what you have in mind, but do not sin through proud speech. (Sir. 20:11–12)

This brings us back to sacred stillness, or *hesychia*. This Greek word is used in Scripture. "But we exhort you, brethren, to do so more and more, to aspire to live *quietly*, to mind your own affairs, and to work with your hands, as we charged you" (1 Thess. 4:10–11). You will perhaps remember: the word means keeping quiet, holding one's peace, to rest, and to cease. Monastics of the Christian East picked up on this and, as a spiritual practice, hesychia reached its greatest expression in a fourteenth-century movement championed by St. Gregory Palamas and the monks of Mount Athos. But sacred stillness is not only for vowed monastics. St. Francis would have this gift present in each of our lives.

Next, in this Admonition, Francis wants to address the problem of boasting. He teaches: "Beware those servants of God who do not protect the good things of God 'in an honest and good heart' (Lk. 8:15), and do not show them to others by what they do. Those who instead aim to show off with words 'have their reward' (Matt. 6:2), and anyone hearing them will receive very little fruit." It is one thing to spread the good news to build others up. This is valid testimony. It is quite another to share what God has done in our lives with the subtle desire to gain attention for ourselves.

In addressing the Jewish Christians, who boasted of their heritage to the exclusion of the Gentiles, St. Paul says, "Then what becomes of our boasting? It is excluded" (Rom. 3:27). James says even more radically, "As it is, you boast in your arrogance. All such boasting is evil" (Jas. 4:16). Just don't do it. What sort of boasting is allowed? St. Paul says, "Let him who boasts, boast of the Lord" (2 Cor. 10:17).

Boasting isn't the only kind of speech that's bad for us. So, too, is gossip: speaking to others about other people in an unhelpful way. Gossip might say what is true, but to the wrong person, and in the wrong spirit. St. Francis was convinced that this was the greatest danger to the continuation of his new community. He called gossipers murderers and said that disaster awaited the community if such gossiping wasn't stopped.

I once did a recording called *Wisdom*. It focused largely on Sirach and Wisdom from the Bible. I was blessed and challenged by what I learned. Sirach says rather completely regarding repeating gossip,

Have you heard a word? Let it die with you. Be brave!
It will not make you burst! With such a word a fool will
suffer pangs like a woman in labor with a child. Like an
arrow stuck in the flesh of the thigh, so is a word inside
a fool. Question a friend, perhaps he did not do it; but if
he did anything, so that he may do it no more. Question
a neighbor, perhaps he did not say it; but if he said it,
so that he may not say it again. Question a friend, for
often it is slander; so do not believe everything you hear.
A person may make a slip without intending it. Who has
never sinned with his tongue? (Sir. 19:10–16)

This speaks to both intention and practice.

This is all good, and we know we should, but how do we get
there? How do we achieve these virtuous goals? The answer is
perhaps deceptively simple, but not easy. To put it plainly, *be
quiet!* As the saying goes, put a sock in it. This is often hard. We
feel that we will burst if we cannot talk.

The Desert Fathers offered a simple but astonishingly simple
solution: "They said of Abba Agatho that for three years he
kept a pebble in his mouth to teach him silence." Sometimes
you have to use an external means to help. Or perhaps another
answer is to ask a loved one to remind us when we are too
talkative. Or tie a string around a finger, like many older folks
used to do to remind them of something important often
forgotten. I actually placed a stone in my mouth a few times
early in my monastic life. It reminded me to keep my words
holy every time I removed it to engage in necessary speech.

In our monastic community, we do this by having "places
and times of silence." We keep The Grand Silence from the end
of Night Prayer at the close of the day until Morning Prayer the
next. We keep general silence until noon each day. If we have
to talk, we try to do so in a quiet way. Throughout the rest of the
day, we speak only in order to edify one another. We also keep

general silence in the chapel, the refectory (monastic dining room), and throughout the corridors. And we recognize that if the drapes are drawn in the hermitage, we do not disturb the person inside. We break silence a lot, but are convinced that regardless of our human failing in keeping it, silence is a goal worth retaining. It can be realized by the grace of Jesus Christ.

How can this apply to people who don't live in a monastic community? First, find times and places for silence in your household, wherever you live. Keep quiet times in the mornings, or prayer before bedtime. Turn things off. Listen to the Holy Spirit. Keep silence in your parish worship space. Learn to speak less but say more. Be confident, but not boastful. These are just some of the lessons from this Admonition.

Admonition 22
True Correction

ST. FRANCIS WROTE:

Blessed are the servants of God who can accept blame, accusation, or punishment from others as patiently as if it were coming from themselves. Blessed are the servants of God who obey quietly when they are corrected, confess their fault humbly, and make amends cheerfully. Blessed are the servants of God who are in no hurry to make excuses, but accept the embarrassment and blame for some fault they did not commit.

My mind is blown when I read this Admonition. Bearing the blame for something we didn't do is outside the realm of reality for most of us. Yet most of the great saints teach this. Let's peel the onion back on this one to perhaps understand what Francis is talking about and why he says it.

It's hard to be corrected. It's embarrassing, even when the person correcting us tries to be gentle and kind. We tend to offer excuses for our bad behavior. Or we tend to blame someone or something else for our actions. Plus, it's exceptionally hard to be blamed for something we are convinced we didn't do. This Admonition really cuts against the grain of what most modern people, even people of faith, are willing to do.

When I was young, I didn't always receive correction well. I was childish. Later on, I learned to take correction a bit more constructively. My spiritual father often challenged my ideas and gave me positive and helpful counsel on how to overcome a shortcoming, a sin, or maybe just a wrong or incomplete idea. My bishop has gently corrected me in talks where I asked him a question about a point. These are always helpful, though I still feel a bit foolish when I am wrong about something. But news flash: We are all wrong about something sometimes!

I am reminded of countless conferences with new monastics. We practice monastic confession, which is distinct from sacramental confession. With sacramental confession, we confess our actual sins to an ordained presbyter of the church. In monastic confession, we confess not only our actual sins but also our temptations, our thoughts, to our monastic spiritual father or mother. We also do this publicly when appropriate.

When we do this rightly we easily and rather quickly lay our thoughts before our spiritual father or mother, elder, or spiritual director. We make no excuses. We humbly lay our thoughts and failings before an experienced elder who has walked the way before us in monastic community living. We receive their input and correction humbly and without resistance, and we try our best to put it into practice. When we do this wrongly we hem and haw and beat around the bush. We make excuses, we try to justify ourselves, and we rationalize our failings. Sometimes we just overthink it and end up wound in a knot. It's usually awkward, uncomfortable, and downright painful. Plus, it takes a lot longer! Afterward, we don't really try to implement the correction and direction that was offered out of love. The entire procedure falls short of the goal: real humility before Jesus in a mediated way in a community of faith by people who are more experienced than we are, and genuinely care for us.

The Desert Fathers and Mothers developed the practice into a fine spiritual art. St. Benedict sums it up in chapter 4 of his Rule when he says, "As soon as wrongful thoughts come into your heart, dash them against Christ and disclose them to your spiritual father." And, "Every day with tears and sighs confess your past sins to God in prayer." Another Desert Father, Abba Poemen, said, "In my opinion, non-silence means not being silent in [manifesting] one's thoughts." There are entire chapters about this in the various editions of their wisdom and sayings, and the letters of great monastic saints who spread monasticism across the Christian world.

St. Francis says, "Blessed are the servants of God who are in no hurry to make excuses, but accept the embarrassment and blame for some fault they did not commit." So how then should we respond to correction, even when it is apparently unjust? As Abba Poemen said—and St. Dorotheus of Gaza, and many others—when we are unjustly accused, perhaps even in anger, we are not to become defensive. We are to take responsibility for what we may have done to provoke the response. Was it something we said or did, perhaps even in the distant past? Was it an attitude, or a countenance, that put them off? Or perhaps we offended someone else, and God is using this encounter to get our attention. Whatever it may be, we are supposed to not get angry with those who are angry with us. Most especially, we do not blame them. Dorotheus of Gaza even says that this is absolutely essential to learn if we are to live in community peacefully with others.

The next step is also important. St. Dorotheus teaches us to correct others, but to do so without anger or blame. He even says that a failure in correction is a failure in charity to that brother or sister. But it must be done without ego or blame. It cannot be an attempt to justify our opinion or position on a matter. It must be done out of love. It must be done without anger, self-justification, or vengeance. It must be completely self-giving and selfless. That is the key. But it isn't easy until we substantially die to our old self, are born again in the Spirit, and rise a new childlike person in Christ.

It is also practical, and Jesus gives practical advice on the process of how to do this with others. Jesus teaches us to go to those with whom we need to be reconciled privately, one on one. If they don't receive it, take others who have had the same trouble and talk to them. Last, bring in community or church authority. Many people jump to the last step, and shortcut the healing. Jesus clearly says,

> If your brother sins against you, go and tell him his fault, between you and him alone. If he listens to you, you have gained your brother. But if he does not listen, take one or two others along with you, that every word may be confirmed by the evidence of two or three witnesses. If he refuses to listen to them, tell it to the church; and if he refuses to listen even to the church, let him be to you as a Gentile and a tax collector. Truly, I say to you, whatever you bind on earth shall be bound in heaven, and whatever you loose on earth shall be loosed in heaven. (Matt. 18:15–18)

Even more, when we talk to others we do not accuse or blame them. We simply say without anger, "When you do this or that, it makes us feel bad, and understand that it is contrary to our community way of life." We share our feelings and understandings. We do not accuse. We do not blame. We try to heal.

How do we accomplish this? Human will alone is a good start, but ultimately it cannot accomplish this. It must come by grace. It is a gift. Only Jesus empowers us through the Holy Spirit to live this remarkably high gospel ideal. When the Holy Spirit is actively stirred up in our life, then Jesus himself is living within us and assisting us to fulfill this teaching. Religion alone cannot do it. Spirituality alone cannot do it. We need both the inside and the outside working in an integrated harmony that only Jesus can bring to fulfill this high calling.

Admonition 23
True Humility

ST. FRANCIS WROTE:

Blessed are those servants who are just as unassuming among those they lead as they are among those who lead them. Blessed are the servants of God who are always willing to be corrected. "The faithful and wise servant" (Matt. 24:45) is the one who is quick to punish himself for his offenses, with contrition on the inside, and on the outside by confession and making reparation.

B lessed are those servants who are just as unassuming among those they lead as they are among those who lead them." We all like this one, especially if we are not in leadership. We like our leaders to be examples of servant leadership. All of us respond better to those who lead by example than to those who try to lead by words alone. If words are first proved by example we take them more seriously.

This requires humility on the part of the leader. St. Benedict says,

> Furthermore, anyone who receives the name of abbot is to lead his disciples by a twofold teaching: he must point out to them all that is good and holy more by example than by words, proposing the commandments of the Lord to receptive disciples with words, but demonstrating

God's instructions to the stubborn and the dull by a living example. Again, if he teaches his disciples that something is not to be done, then neither must he do it, lest after preaching to others, he himself be found reprobate and God some day call to him in his sin: How is it that you repeat my just commands and mouth my covenant when you hate discipline and toss my words behind you? And also this: How is it that you can see a splinter in your brother's eye, and never notice the plank in your own? The abbot should avoid all favoritism in the monastery. (RB 2.11–16)

Each of us has different gifts from God. We each play different roles in our communities and parishes as well. Each gift and each role is important. This means we are all to walk humbly before God and each other, willing to recognize, respect, and love the gifts of God in others. We are one body, and none of us is really complete without appreciating, and working in harmony with, the other. I need you, and you need me.

St. Francis continues with something no less challenging: "Always willing to be corrected." Really? Yes! This Admonition represents an attitude completely countercultural to our typical modern way of relating with each other. We are taught to assert ourselves, to look out for our own rights. Francis reminds us that Jesus teaches us to allow our selves to die, so that we might discover a completely new and liberating life in him. Only then do we discover the far more expansive rights of fully becoming a child of God. This treatment on how well we handle correction is one area where that death to the old self is tested. It's where the rubber meets the road.

When I was a boy, I loved to swim. It was said of me that I spent more time swimming underwater than on the surface. It was true. I loved to swim underwater to discover an entirely new world just below the surface. But when I was enrolled for swimming lessons at the YMCA my instructor tried to teach me how to become a surface swimmer. I didn't much like it. All I remember was that it was far more work, and I tended to swallow water every time I raised my mouth above the surface to breathe. When the instructor corrected me from the side of the pool, I was humiliated. I went home and never returned. I lost all enthusiasm for the class. But the instructor wasn't wrong. I was! And I missed the opportunity of becoming a skilled swimmer. I still can't swim well today.

This has been true in other areas of my life too. I suspect it's true of most of us to some degree. Yet by doing so, we rob ourselves and others of having our God-given gifts perfected by those who have the authority and to guide us. Most of us hate correction. Yet, we love to correct, or at least criticize, others, regardless of our authority to do so! Ironically, instead of making us more sensitive at helping others, when we regularly resist correction we tend to correct other people badly.

Proverbs 12:1 says, "He who loves correction loves knowledge, but he who hates reproof is stupid" (NAB). And Proverbs 13:1 says, "A wise son loves correction, but the senseless one heeds no rebuke" (NAB). Sirach teaches, "He who hates correction walks the sinner's path, but he who fears the LORD repents in his heart" (Sirach 21:6 NAB). This submission to correction empowers us to correct those under our authority in a healthy and life-giving way. A leader can only lead well when they are good followers.

St. Paul says, "Brothers, even if a person is caught in some transgression, you who are spiritual should correct that one in a gentle spirit, looking to yourself, so that you also may not be tempted" (Gal. 6:1 NAB). And to Timothy, his spiritual son in Christ, he says, "Avoid foolish and ignorant debates, for you know that they breed quarrels. A slave of the Lord should not quarrel, but should be gentle with everyone, able to teach, tolerant, correcting opponents with kindness. It may be that

God will grant them repentance that leads to knowledge of the truth, and that they may return to their senses out of the devil's snare, where they are entrapped by him, for his will" (2 Tim. 2:21–26 NAB). The Greek for "correcting" is *paideuō*, meaning to chastise, teach, or instruct. It is similar to the word used by Paul for the Law, *paidagogos*—meaning a schoolmaster, tutor, or disciplinarian. Its purpose is to educate, not to punish.

But we don't correct according to our human plans or designs. We correct according to the plan and design of God, to which we have first humbly submitted. Paul says we use both apostolic tradition and Sacred Scripture to guide our spiritual and moral compass. "But as for you, continue in what you have learned and have firmly believed, knowing from whom you learned it and how from childhood you have been acquainted with the sacred writings which are able to instruct you for salvation through faith in Christ Jesus. All scripture is inspired by God and profitable for teaching, for reproof, for correction, and for training in righteousness, that the man of God may be complete, equipped for every good work" (2 Tim. 3:14–17).

We also don't correct according to our personal opinions, our own spiritual likes and dislikes. In my community, we use the broader apostolic tradition of the church, and the monastic and Franciscan traditions as well. It must be done personally, but it isn't according to the personal whim of the superior. It also usually means to correct one thing at a time, not everything at once. Wisdom says, "Therefore you rebuke offenders little by little, warn them, and remind them of the sins they are committing, that they may abandon their wickedness and believe in you, O LORD!" (Wis. 12:2 NAB). I am always stunned and amazed by how God corrects me of sin little by little. Otherwise, I would be overwhelmed by the immensity of my foolishness and sin. I am also amazed at how God only allows me to see one glimpse at a time the full view of the glory we share in, both now and in eternity.

St. Francis says that we should be eager for instruction and correction. This expands on what we find in Scripture: "Frequent the company of the elders; whoever is wise, stay close to him. Be eager to hear every godly discourse; let no wise saying escape you. If you see a man of prudence, seek him out; let your feet wear away his doorstep! Reflect on the precepts of the LORD, let his commandments be your constant meditation; Then he will enlighten your mind, and the wisdom you desire he will grant" (Sir. 6:34–37 NAB).

When I first found my spiritual father, Fr. Martin Wolter, OFM, I met with him almost daily for months. I took a room and moved to the Franciscan retreat center where he was living. I was eager to learn, and even to be corrected, to find God's wisdom for my life in ideals and practice. Gradually, we tapered off to meeting weekly, and only less frequently as both he and I got older. I listened to him with great eagerness and joy. His brother friars kidded him about his calling it "one-hour Martinizing"! He could go on for an hour before getting to the point. But I didn't care. He always did get to the point, and it was always good. I was learning more about Jesus, Francis, and the church. Eventually I more fully embraced all three!

This doesn't mean he was perfect. Far from it! Fr. Martin could be downright aggravating. He caught every little mistake in my writings, or the deviations in my public appearances. He could be demanding, judgmental, and nitpicky when traveling. Sometimes others who knew us both wondered why I was so loyal to him. The reason was clear: Despite his obvious human failings, Jesus spoke to me time after time in nothing short of supernatural ways through Fr. Martin. When I submitted to his guidance and correction I prospered. When I did not, I didn't. But in the end, I benefited more than I can express in words by approaching him with love and respect as my spiritual father.

The Letter to the Hebrews says,

> "My son, do not regard lightly the discipline of the Lord,
> nor lose courage when you are punished by him.
> For the Lord disciplines him whom he loves,
> and chastises every son whom he receives."

It is for discipline that you have to endure. God is treating you as sons; for what son is there whom his father does not discipline? If you are left without discipline, in which all have participated, then you are illegitimate children and not sons. Besides this, we have had earthly fathers to discipline us and we respected them. Shall we not much more be subject to the Father of spirits and live? For they disciplined us for a short time at their pleasure, but he disciplines us for our good, that we may share his holiness. For the moment all discipline seems painful rather than pleasant; later it yields the peaceful fruit of righteousness to those who have been trained by it. (Heb. 12:5–11)

This is what Francis gets at with this Admonition: we must be eager for correction. It might be a bit painful at the time, but in the long run it makes us better. The correction might be offered well or imperfectly from very human teachers, but if we accept it to find the kernel of wisdom in their teaching, we benefit greatly.

Admonitions 24 & 25
True Love

⟨⟨⟨ ST. FRANCIS WROTE:

Blessed are the servants of God who love their brothers and sisters as much when they are sick as when they are well.

(Admonition 24)

This simple, short Admonition puts some further flesh on the bones. We'll take Admonition 24, first, followed by 25. They are both about "True Love."

I was recently very sick in bed, then in the hospital. I was facing death. It is an understatement to say that I was doing a lot of soul-searching about my past, and my future. Close friends and community members came to visit. I cannot tell you how meaningful that was for me. They came just to be with me. They prayed a bit, but mainly they just sat with me for a time. They didn't talk much, for that would have been too painful for me. They were simply present. They were gentle. They were kind. It was powerful. I was amazed at how meaningful it is to be visited when very, very sick.

This is why the early church always had ordained men and deaconesses to minster to bedridden men and women respectively. This was private, but powerful. It was gentle, but it brought the strength that only God can bring. Plus, it ministers to the ministers more than words can tell. I can tell story after story of how encouraged I was after ministering to the sick. But the words would fall short of the love that was brought into my heart by God's working through the sick or the poor.

But visiting the sick can be uncomfortable. They can be agitated or unresponsive. They can smell. We sometimes worry about contracting whatever illness they have. However, the truth remains that visiting the sick is a key component of Christian lifestyle and ministry. St. Francis addresses these objections. He does so mainly on the level of usefulness. He says, "Blessed are the servants of God who love their brothers and sisters as much when they are sick as when they are well." The sick are out of the apparent "workforce" of a community. They are "useless" on the practical level. Therefore, we cannot get anything useful from them.

The Rule of St. Benedict addresses ministering to the sick. It is simply assumed that it is done, but it does not assume that it will be done well, so it offers specifics. Chapter 36 teaches,

> Care of the sick must rank above and before all else, so that they may truly be served as Christ, for he said: "I was sick and you visited me," and, "What you did for one of these least brothers you did for me." Let the sick on their part bear in mind that they are served out of honor for God, and let them not by their excessive demands distress their brothers who serve them. Still, sick brothers must be patiently borne with, because serving them leads to a greater reward. Consequently, the abbot should be extremely careful that they suffer no neglect. Let a separate room be designated for the sick, and let them be served by an attendant who is God-fearing, attentive and concerned. The sick may take baths whenever it is advisable, but the healthy, and especially the young, should receive permission less readily. Moreover, to

regain their strength, the sick who are very weak may eat meat, but when their health improves, they should all abstain from meat as usual. The abbot must take the greatest care that cellarers and those who serve the sick do not neglect them, for the shortcomings of disciples are his responsibility.

The cellarer, who's in charge of the physical goods of the monastery, is supposed to show special care for the sick. The sick are exempted from kitchen duty. They are given red meat, when others are not allowed to eat it. They are given more wine, if it would benefit them to have more. They are freed from having to do any strenuous work, or even work of any kind, while they are sick. All of this summarizes the monastic tradition as it was before the time of St. Benedict. It is both sacrificial and practical. Care for the sick was simply a part of daily life.

We respond to the sick as followers of Jesus Christ. It is the teaching of Jesus that inspires the entire Rule of St. Benedict. So there remains no excuse not to care for them or to leave them in loneliness. "Is any among you sick? Let him call for the elders of the church, and let them pray over him, anointing him with oil in the name of the Lord; and the prayer of faith will save the sick man, and the Lord will raise him up; and if he has committed sins, he will be forgiven," says St. James (5:14–16).

The biblical word for "sick" is *kamno*, meaning "ill, weary, and faint." The word for "save" is *sōzō*, meaning "to save, make whole, and heal." But this also involves forgiveness. The word here for "forgiven" is *aphiemi*, meaning "to leave, send away, or forsake." When we minster to the sick we bring the forgiveness of Jesus. This is done sacramentally through bishops and presbyters, and personally through deacons and lay ministers.

Forgiveness unlocks the power of the Spirit in our life. It binds or looses. It frees or imprisons. When we offer forgiveness, we are forgiven. When we withhold forgiveness when it should be offered, we bind up other people and ourselves. Forgiveness is a huge part of healing. When we forgive, we heal the soul first, and then the body. When the soul is healed through mercy and forgiveness, then many of the stress and tensions of the body are healed. Modern medicine is now telling us that these stresses and tensions can cause and contribute to a wide array of physical ailments, including things like cancer, that can actually kill us. The point is: forgiveness and healing go together.

ST. FRANCIS WROTE:

Blessed are the servants of God who love and respect their brothers and sisters as much when they are absent as when they are present, and who do not say anything behind their backs that they could not or would not say charitably in their presence.

(Admonition 25)

Admonition 25 reminds us how easy it is to talk about someone who is not looking at you face-to-face, eyeball-to-eyeball. We should never say in someone's absence what we would not say to them in person. On social media, it is too easy to post a rant or accusation with very little to substantiate it. We can speak with anger and have disregard for mutual respect because the people or organizations we are gossiping about, or even slandering, aren't right there to respond. And even if they are, such exchanges in the typical writing style of social media do not lend themselves to good communication. It is usually just polemics, not true dialogue. Instead of bringing people closer together, these exchanges can push us further apart.

This polarization is a great danger. The late Fr. Benedict Groeschel, CFR, once shared with me that he believed our culture is more divided now than it has been since the Civil War. The problem is that there is no geographical line to separate us. We are all mixed together at every level. We interact more, and the more we do so in anger, the further apart we are pushed.

We have already discussed gossip and slander in these lessons from St. Francis. You might remember my view: gossip is basically saying the true thing to the wrong person; slander is saying something false to the wrong person. Both are sins. And far more of us engage in these sins than we like to admit. Sirach says of both:

> He who gloats over evil will meet with evil, and he who repeats an evil report has no sense. Never repeat gossip, and you will not be reviled. Tell nothing to friend or foe; if you have a fault, reveal it not, for he who hears it will hold it against you, and in time become your enemy. Let anything you hear die within you; be assured it will not make you burst. When a fool hears something, he is in labor, like a woman giving birth to a child. Like an arrow lodged in a man's thigh is gossip in the breast of a fool. Admonish your friend—he may not have done it; and if he did, that he may not do it again. Admonish your neighbor—he may not have said it; and if he did, that he may not say it again. Admonish your friend—often it may be slander; every story you must not believe. Then, too, a man can slip and not mean it; who has not sinned

with his tongue? Admonish your neighbor before you break with him; thus will you fulfill the law of the Most High. (Sir. 19:5–16 NAB)

Both gossip and slander are terrible.

St. Francis was harsh, too, when it comes to gossips and slanderers. He described them as murderers and said that they would destroy the Franciscan order from within if they were not stopped. It is one of the few times we hear Francis recommend physical punishment. Gossips kill other people through words.

There was a time early in our community history when we also had to address gossip. It seemed that otherwise good Christians simply loved to gossip about people and things. This led to division. It threatened our new community. Why do we do this? I am convinced that gossip makes us feel somehow superior to the people we are gossiping about. It stems from our own lack of confidence in who we really are in Christ. Lacking a humble self-confidence in Christ, we prop ourselves up through egotism and either criticize others openly or gossip about them privately to make ourselves feel more important. The cure is really having faith in the truth that we are created in God's image and likeness, and after turning from God and losing his likeness, still being loved enough by God to send his Son to rescue us and restore us to his likeness.

So we must love, not only those who we like or agree with, or who are useful to a given ministry or work of ours, but also those who are not. We must truly love and care for those who are sick. We must also love those who are absent from us, and not part of our active orbit. This is especially true with our modern use of social media: we lose track of real friends and people in real time. Take some time to visit the sick, regardless of their ability to reward you. Be careful how you talk about people who aren't physically present. These are some of the lessons of St. Francis from these two Admonitions on true love.

Admonition 26
Be Respectful of Clergy

ST. FRANCIS WROTE:

Blessed are servants of God who have confidence in priests who live according to the laws of the holy Roman Church. Woe to those who despise them. Even if they fall into sin, we should not pass judgment, because "it is the Lord who judges" (1 Cor. 4:4). They are in an important position because they have responsibility for the body and blood of our Lord Jesus Christ, which they receive and they alone may administer to others. So one who sins against the clergy commits a greater crime than if he sinned against anyone else in the world.

Francis was a Middle Ages revivalist. He preached the gospel of Jesus Christ to tens of thousands. He brought about their conversion too. His evangelistic zeal spread like wildfire and attracted thousands who were trained to do the same. Franciscan history is filled with dynamic preachers unlike anything we usually see in today's mainstream Orthodox or Catholic churches.

His was an age of Spirit-led revival and renewal. And Francis was not alone. There were many others from among his early followers who were called to give their lives completely to

Christ. One of the earmarks of their movement was embracing a radical gospel poverty and simplicity of life, in stark contrast to the corrupt clergy of the Roman Church of the day. Together with St. Dominic (founder of the Dominican order), St. Francis remained within the church and renewed it from within. They saw corruption and a turning away from the faith and its holy practices and traditions, and they worked assiduously to rebuild.

Francis practiced a poverty that was greater than that of any of the other reform groups. He and Dominic also embraced a humble obedience to the Roman Catholic Church that was extraordinary. This is what set them apart from others—and perhaps what drew many people to follow them. They were extraordinarily successful. By the end of Francis's short life there were some five thousand brothers, hundreds of sisters, and tens of thousands of laypeople associated with the Franciscan movement as penitents, or Third Order members. Dante would say seventy-five years later that the Franciscans had literally carpeted Europe!

This Admonition addresses St. Francis's relationship to the clergy. In short, he recommends converting the clergy by serving them in humble obedience. There are numerous stories in the early accounts of Francis's life and ministry that demonstrate how the hard hearts of corrupt clergy were softened and turned back to Jesus through the humble example of him and his friars, even when they faced bodily harm through the persecution the clergy orchestrated. And it worked! Francis reached for a higher accomplishment and reward than the low-hanging fruit of sectarianism and division in the name of so-called purity of the gospel, which characterized many sectarian reform movements, such as the Cathars and Waldensians (whom we discussed earlier), simultaneous with Francis.

Jesus himself gives us the first model for such obedience to religious authority. Jesus says, "The scribes and the Pharisees sit on Moses' seat; so practice and observe whatever they tell you, but not what they do; for they preach, but do not practice" (Matt. 23:2–3). Authority was given by the Father to Jesus, and by Jesus to the apostles: "All authority in heaven and on earth has been given to me. Go therefore and make disciples of all nations, baptizing them in the name of the Father and of the Son and of the Holy Spirit, teaching them to observe all that I have commanded you; and lo, I am with you always, to the close of the age" (Matt. 28:18–20). This apostolic authority is passed from the apostles to their successors. "And when they had appointed elders for them in every church, with prayer and fasting, they committed them to the Lord in whom they believed" (Acts 14:23).

St. Paul exhorts Titus to exercise his apostolic authority: "Declare these things; exhort and reprove with all authority. Let no one disregard you" (Tit. 2:15). This succession in the early church was the test for authenticity of the teaching of Jesus. There wasn't yet a canon, or compilation of New Testament Scripture, and even the list of the books of Jewish Scriptures was not yet set in concrete. The only objective link they had with the historical Christ was through those who were apostles, and through their successors, the bishops. This was seen in a special way as being preserved in the bishop of Rome, who succeeded St. Peter, to whom Jesus has given the first place, the primacy, and the keys to the heavenly kingdom.

What is important to us now—and expressed in this Admonition—is how we are to relate to local pastors and bishops. It can even affect how Catholics relate to particular popes. What do we do when our pastor isn't open to what we think would renew our parish? Or what if he is simply unkind, unhelpful, unresponsive? What do we do when our local bishop is less than pastoral, and seems to maintain a leadership style from ages long past? This is especially important in the face of scandals in the church. Scandals and corruption may cause us to want to give up and leave. But that isn't what St. Francis taught was best. Those who are inspired by St. Francis today will stick it out and work to fix the problems that are there.

Francis gives us a challenging answer. It is far too easy to simply break away and start our own faith community or church. Christians have done that too often! He says that we are to remain humble and obedient regarding their office, though we may not always agree with their personal example, or even particular positions that are officially orthodox but, we believe, pastorally ineffective. This is countercultural.

There are over four thousand denominations in America alone. This plethora attests not only to the wonderful diversity of the people of God but also to the scandal of division and disunity. The breakaway pattern continues. Even in our own little country town closest to Little Portion Hermitage, we have witnessed many new congregations crop up from churches that were once, and still try to be, Spirit-filled faith communities. The division continues. It has been going on since the early church.

Today we also face the phenomenon of the megachurch movement. There are many criticisms and praises of it. Some object to a lowering of the bar of orthodoxy in order to reach a larger group of Westerners who have already been affected by the secularism of our time. Specifically, the shallow content and emotionalism of contemporary music, or the lightweight, emotionally charged preaching, or the lack of full sacramental ministry is often used to illustrate this trend. I tend, instead, to see the things they do well, and bring those into our Catholic experience in a way that avoids the theological, ecclesial, and spiritual problems to which they have sometimes succumbed.

The way to bring about renewal in the church, Francis says here, and by his lifelong example, is not by breaking away from a church or pastor when we disagree with him or find him less than helpful. Staying in full communion and doing what we can do to help right where we are is the way to bring about renewal. We do this by personally participating at Mass in a full and active way. We sing and lift our minds and hearts through real worship. We listen to the proclamation of the Word in Scripture and preaching, and we support our preachers with our eyes, and our smiles, and maybe even an occasional "Amen!" Then we go forward to receive Jesus in complete awe and wonder.

So Francis has much to teach us about renewing the church in any era. We all face different issues that are unique to our culture, time, and place, but the universal principle remains the same: we renew the church from within, not by breaking away from her.

Admonition 27
Virtue and Vice

ST. FRANCIS WROTE:

Where there is love and wisdom, there is no fear or ignorance. Where there is patience and humility, there is not anger or annoyance. Where there is poverty and joy, there is no materialism or greed. Where there is peace and contemplation, there is not fussiness or restlessness. Where there is the fear of God in the house, no enemy may enter. Where there is mercy and discernment, there are neither excessive expectations or hard hearts.

This authentic writing of St. Francis is remarkably similar to the famous "Peace Prayer" of Francis. But we know that the Peace Prayer wasn't written until World War I at the earliest. It authentically captures the spirit of St. Francis, but it cannot be found in the universally accepted authentic writings of the saint.

This Admonition reads like a beautiful poem to virtue. It is brief but comprehensive. In many ways, it summarizes what we have meditated on in the preceding Admonitions. And yet it would require a book unto itself to fully address this one alone.

Let's begin with the first line: "Where there is love and wisdom, there is no fear or ignorance." Scripture says, "There is no fear in love, but perfect love casts out fear. For fear has to do with punishment, and he who fears is not perfected in love. We love, because he first loved us" (1 John 4:18–19). And yet Scripture also says, "The fear of the LORD is the beginning of wisdom, and the knowledge of the Holy One is insight" (Prov. 9:10). What does this apparent contradiction really mean?

A healthy fear of the Lord is simply awe and wonder. Even Jesus had a healthy fear of God the Father. "In the days of his flesh, Jesus offered up prayers and supplications, with loud cries and tears, to him who was able to save him from death, and he was heard for his godly fear" (Heb. 5:7). The Greek here for godly fear here is *eulabeia*, from a root meaning devout, pious, and religious.

But then there is an unhealthy fear. Scripture says, "For God hath not given us the spirit of fear: but of power, and of love, and of sobriety" (2 Tim. 1:7 Douay-Rheims). The Greek for "fear" is *deilia*, meaning timidity and lack of confidence. Healthy fear of God empowers us forward toward divine knowledge and wisdom. Unhealthy fear cripples and paralyzes.

Next, let's examine the second line of this Admonition: "Where there is patience and humility, there is not anger or annoyance." Authentic humility means to bring our false self, with its displaced ego and, through a healthy attachment to the cross, let that false self go. Only then can we become a new creation in Christ. All of those unhealthy attachments to little things in our lives will lead to attachments to bigger, unhealthier things. And as these attachments are threatened, we easily become angry and annoyed. If we become free of these attachments through humility, we become free.

Humility also brings patience. When we stop trying to control other things, people, or situations, we are able to let God be in control. This results with a patience that brings us a real inner peace and calm. It also brings us joy.

The third line says this: "Where there is poverty and joy, there is no materialism or greed." For St. Francis, this means that when we let go of other things, and let God guide us through the cross and resurrection of Jesus, we are able to embrace a gospel poverty that gives us greater wealth than the world can ever give us. It also brings us a joy that comes from being relieved of the terrible burden of carrying around our old self.

Materialism is toxic. Possessions often possess us, and we are consumed by our consumerism. This steals from the truly poor, and eventually robs us of greater spiritual wealth. The desire to possess things eats people up. It opens the way to anger and bitterness. Greed is the desire to possess and control things, people, and situations. When you don't get the stuff you want, or the control you want, you get angry. It first manifests as frustration. Then it blossoms into anger. And when anger isn't healed it hides in the inner recesses of the heart and soul as bitterness. That bitterness poisons everything it touches. It poisons every relationship and every situation. A bitter soul always sees the negative. The glass is always half empty, and never half full.

Line four of the Admonition then says, "Where there is peace and contemplation, there is not fussiness or restlessness." In most classical treatments of prayer, contemplation is the last stage. It follows reading sacred texts, praying them, and deeply meditating on them through the imagination. Contemplation is an inner experience of God in a way that builds on ideas and words but is beyond them. It simply *is* with the One who *Is*. It is a perfect rest from our religious or secular labors.

No one can relate to this description if they haven't experienced it, or at least tasted it in an initiatory way that stirs a longing for it. It also cannot be obtained by study or ascetical labor, though both can lead to it. It is like setting a table for a special guest. We can labor to set the table, but it is up to the guest to actually show up. And when they do, we are filled with fulfillment and joy; we can simply rest with the guest and enjoy a meal. That guest is God. Setting the table is the active life. The arrival of the Guest is contemplation. The meal is the Supper of the Lamb.

When we experience this, we are like what St. Francis described elsewhere in his writings: "When we have no house, we are everywhere at home." And, "When we have no property to defend, we can be at peace with everyone." When you have this contemplative poverty you have dispassion and peace, regardless of what happens to you. You lose your restlessness. In a very real way, you are satisfied everywhere you go.

This brings us to the fifth sentence in this incredible Admonition: "Where there is the fear of God in the house, no enemy may enter." Let's not rush through this one. St. Francis is making a slight transition here.

The peace of contemplation is real, and it is substantial, but that doesn't mean there is no more spiritual warfare in the life of the follower of Jesus. Even Jesus went through such battles. We know that he was sorely tempted after his forty-day fast and prayer in the desert. He was tempted to three things: (1) physical food after intense hunger, (2) power and authority if he would worship Satan, and (3) miraculous powers if he would tempt God (Lk. 4:1–12). Jesus defeated all these temptations. How? The devil quoted Scripture wrongly, and out of context. Jesus defeated the devil by knowing the real truth and quoting Scripture rightly. After that happened, Scripture says, "When the devil had ended every temptation, he departed from him until an opportune time" (Lk. 4:13). The Greek for "opportune time" is *kairos*, and means due time, or opportunity. So it implies that he came back! Jesus had to resist temptation repeatedly. Jesus was tempted as we are, but he did not give in to it. "We have not a high priest who is unable to sympathize with our weaknesses, but one who in every respect has been tempted as we are, yet without sinning. Let us then with confidence draw near to the throne of grace" (Heb. 4:15–16).

Spiritual warfare is expressed and understood in our praying of the psalms that refer to external warfare. There are countless psalms celebrating God's victory over enemies. For the Christian, the enemy is spiritual. It is sin and negativity that we are tempted to give in to. For us, Jesus is the victor. Jesus promises, "In the world you have tribulation; but be of good cheer, I have overcome the world" (John 16:33). We share in that victory. "I write to you, young men, because you are strong, and the word of God abides in you, and you have overcome the evil one" (1 John 2:14).

St. Paul speaks of the "armor of God" given us by Jesus Christ (Eph. 6:13–17). We have resources galore in these daily battles of ours. Ultimately, the defeat of evil is done through the blood of Jesus Christ: "For the accuser of our brethren has been thrown down, who accuses them day and night before our God. And they have conquered him by the blood of the Lamb and by the word of their testimony, for they loved not their lives even unto death" (Rev. 12:10–11).

And now we turn to the final sentence of this penultimate Admonition: "Where there is mercy and discernment, there are neither excessive expectations or hard hearts." St. Francis knows that prudence and discernment are tools to avoid excess. The Scriptures warn against excess: "For such a one this punishment by the majority is enough; so you should rather turn to forgive and comfort him, or he may be overwhelmed by excessive sorrow" (2 Cor. 2:6–7). Even a good thing taken to excess can cause harm. "Wine drunk to excess is bitterness of soul, with provocation and stumbling" (Sir. 31:29).

Prudence and discernment involve insight and instruction. "That men may know wisdom and instruction, understand words of insight, receive instruction in wise dealing, righteousness, justice, and equity; that prudence may be given to the simple, knowledge and discretion to the youth," says Proverbs (1:2–4). Notice the connection between prudence and discretion.

Wisdom is also linked to prudence: "I, wisdom, dwell in prudence, and I find knowledge and discretion" (Prov. 8:12). She (Wisdom) also teaches it: "She teaches self-control and prudence" (Wis. 8:17). Conversely, sin precludes it: "But the knowledge of wickedness is not wisdom, nor is there prudence where sinners take counsel" (Sir. 19:22).

Having realistic expectations is also vital. We must have the faith to expect miracles (Mk. 11). But we must have the humility to accept the miracles that God brings. He always works miracles. He always heals. But he might do it in a way differently and deeper than what we initially expect. We must have a vision, for where there is no vision a people perish (Prov. 29:18 KJV). And we boldly approach God, but it is always to his grace and mercy (Heb. 4:16), not our presumptuous and often unrealistic expectations, that we appeal. Knowing the difference is a wisdom that brings us peace in all circumstances.

St. Francis knows from experience that mercy heals harshness. Mercy teaches us to avoid hard hearts. In the New Testament, James says that gentleness—the virtue standing on the other side of harshness—is part of wisdom. "The wisdom from above is first pure, then peaceable, gentle, open to reason, full of mercy and good fruits, without uncertainty or insincerity. And the harvest of righteousness is sown in peace by those who make peace" (Jas. 3:17–18). Harshness is also mentioned in Jude and is linked to a list of other sins. "'All the harsh things which ungodly sinners have spoken against him.' These are grumblers, malcontents, following their own passions, loud-mouthed boasters, flattering people to gain advantage" (Jude 15–16). The word "harsh" comes from the Greek *skleros,* meaning "hard, rough, stern," and refers to things violent, rough, offensive, and intolerable.

These vices can be healed through mercy. Mercy is from the depths of God, and it reaches to the depths of the penitent. Sin separates us from full union with God, others, creation, and even ourselves. It means that God knows us better than ourselves, because he is closer to us than we are to ourselves. As St. Augustine said, "You were in me, but I was not in You." God can forgive us better than we can forgive ourselves, because he is more intimately united with us than we are to ourselves.

Jesus teaches mercy as foundational: "Blessed are the merciful, for they shall obtain mercy" (Matt. 5:7). This means compassion, sympathy, and empathy. It means to have compassion by being within the other. God has mercy on us because he is closer to us than we are to ourselves. He knows us better than we know ourselves. When we have mercy on others we can only be within them fully when we operate in the Holy Spirit, who is within us all. Without Jesus and the indwelling Spirit we simply cannot be merciful.

Mercy manifests the love of God for all people, sinners and saints, in a way that sees not merely the external works of law but the inner works of the heart and soul. He says, "Go and learn what this means, 'I desire mercy, and not sacrifice.' For I came not to call the righteous, but sinners" (Matt. 9:13). It is important to remember that the point of the sacrifices of the law is to bring mercy to God's people. They foreshadow the sacrifice of Jesus on the cross, which is the love of God poured out for each and all of us.

The Catholic Church teaches that when rightly understood there is no dichotomy between justice and mercy. Indeed, justice, when rightly understood and applied, *is* merciful. The principle "eye for eye, and tooth for tooth" is not about getting even. It is about moderating vengeance. In the ancient times, when you killed one of my people, we wiped out your village. The eye-for-an-eye rule is about moderating that knee-jerk reaction of vengeance and establishing a justice that manifests and paves the way for mercy. And it paves the way for the nonresistance and forgiveness taught by Jesus, who completely fulfills the law with love. Jesus says, "You shall love the Lord your God with all your heart, and with all your soul, and with all your mind. This is the great and first commandment. And a second is like it, You shall love your neighbor as yourself. On these two commandments depend all the law and the prophets" (Matt. 22:37–40).

St. Paul adds comprehensively, "Owe no one anything, except to love one another; for he who loves his neighbor has fulfilled the law. The commandments, 'You shall not commit adultery, You shall not kill, You shall not steal, You shall not covet,' and any other commandment, are summed up in this sentence, 'You shall love your neighbor as yourself.' Love does no wrong to a neighbor; therefore love is the fulfilling of the law" (Rom. 13:8–10).

In this beautiful set of axioms in Admonition 27 we find nothing less than a swift summary of all that has come before— of all that is important in our Christian lives. Admonition 27, then, leads us almost effortlessly to the final Admonition.

Admonition 28
Virtue Should Be Concealed or It Will Be Lost

⁓ ST. FRANCIS WROTE:

Blessed are the servants of God who "store up treasures in heaven" (Matt. 6:20), the favors God has given them, and do not want to show them off for what they can get for them now. God will reveal our works to whomever God pleases. Blessed are the servants of God who keep God's marvelous doings to themselves.

M ost of us like to be noticed, or at least appreciated for our talents, skills, and good works—don't we? It seems only natural to want people to see what we do and accomplish. We often feel overlooked by family, work, or even friends. We are often hungry to be noticed. But St. Francis turns this on its head, not to negate positive affirmation, but to direct all affirmation toward the One who really matters, Jesus! Once we are loved and affirmed by God, then human notice is simply a passing thing and can come or go.

So Jesus says, "Thus, when you give alms, sound no trumpet before you, as the hypocrites do in the synagogues and in the streets, that they may be praised by men. Truly, I say to you, they have their reward. But when you give alms, do not let your left hand know what your right hand is doing, so that your alms may be in secret; and your Father who sees in secret will reward you" (Matt. 6:2–4). This is followed by, "And when you pray, you must not be like the hypocrites; for they love to stand and pray in the synagogues and at the street corners, that they may be seen by men. Truly, I say to you, they have their reward. But when you pray, go into your room and shut the door and pray to your Father who is in secret; and your Father who sees in secret will reward you" (Matt. 6:5–6).

This means that God the Father sees everything we do, and he rewards us for everything better than any human can do. He sees us better than we can even see ourselves. He understands us better than we understand ourselves. He is closer to us than we are to ourselves. He can reward us and affirm us better than we can reward and affirm ourselves, or others can do.

St. Paul says something similar when discussing the gifts of the Spirit and our salvation: "The secrets of his heart are disclosed; and so, falling on his face, he will worship God and declare that God is really among you" (1 Cor. 14:25). This applies to Jews and Gentiles, believers and unbelievers. Paul says, "They show that what the law requires is written on their hearts, while their conscience also bears witness and their conflicting thoughts accuse or perhaps excuse them on that day when, according to my gospel, God judges the secrets of men by Christ Jesus" (Rom. 2:15–16).

You see, we are hidden now in Christ. But we will be revealed in him when he comes again. "Set your minds on things that are above, not on things that are on earth. For you have died, and your life is hid with Christ in God. When Christ who is our life appears, then you also will appear with him in glory" (Col. 3:2–4). We are hidden in Christ, but our works are reflected on him. Jesus says, "You are the light of the world. A city set on a hill cannot be hid. Nor do men light a lamp and put it under a bushel, but on a stand, and it gives light to all in the house. Let your light so shine before men, that they may see your good works and give glory to your Father who is in heaven" (Matt. 5:14–16).

This last Admonition is based on much of what has come before in the previous ones. The humility that encourages us to seek glory in the glory of others, and to rejoice in the joys of others, is the foundation on which this last teaching stands.

We are to seek the benefit of others before we seek our own. "In humility count others better than yourselves. Let each of you look not only to his own interests, but also to the interests of others" (Phil. 2:3–4). There is no easy way around this challenge. We are only complete when working in communion with others in Christ. The self finds its fulfillment when it dies through Christ.

St. Francis also implies that some of us suffer when others are affirmed instead of us. No doubt, the ego suffers when not stroked! But since the ego must suffer and die to its old primacy in our life, we can also rejoice in those sufferings. In suffering we share in the suffering of Jesus on the cross. Even though we are unappreciated outwardly, we are affirmed inwardly. Plus, suffering builds character, and makes us stronger. Suffering stirs or destroys faith, and faith causes us to have hope and perseverance. And perseverance strengthens us to reach our goal. Paul says, "More than that, we rejoice in our sufferings, knowing that suffering produces endurance, and endurance produces character, and character produces hope, and hope does not disappoint us, because God's love has been poured into our hearts through the Holy Spirit who has been given to us" (Rom. 5:3–5).

There is an inherent mystical link between the suffering of the cross and the glory of the resurrection. This is why Paul says to the Philippians, "that I may know him and the power of his resurrection, and may share his sufferings, becoming like him in his death, that if possible I may attain the resurrection from the dead" (Phil. 3:10–11). He even goes so far as to say that he makes up what is lacking in the sufferings of Christ on the practical level of the church on earth (Col. 1:24). Our suffering allows us to share in the redemptive suffering of Jesus Christ.

So, are we willing to suffer by not being noticed so that Jesus can be seen in our lives? I must admit that after all these decades I am still working on it. As they say, I am a practicing Catholic precisely because I am still *practicing*! But as the end of my life draws closer, I am hoping and praying I'll be ready for the ultimate concert before the Father, the Son, and the Holy Spirit. Please pray for my unworthy soul. Only Jesus Christ is worthy to be praised.

This is ultimately what the Admonitions of St. Francis are all about. Jesus alone must be our all in all. When we die in him, and say with St. Paul that it is no longer I, but Christ who lives in me, then we are starting to get the hang of what Francis lived and taught.

Conclusion

These are the Admonitions of St. Francis. They are radically countercultural. Yet they can radically remake culture. They might well be part of the answer the world needs in this dark hour. Yet our world still holds the potential for much hope and promise in God's light in the future.

They are blessings for those who are willing to embrace them. But it is not a blessing or happiness that the world teaches. This happiness, this blessing, is much deeper than what is possible through immersing oneself in politics, or culture, or even debates in the church. The happiness and blessing the Admonitions offer can remake us if we dare to let them live in us, and allow them to spread to others, one person at a time.

Francis was called to "repair my house, for as you can see, it is falling to ruin." And it worked! Francis took a personal approach that went far beyond just preaching to crowds. He started one person at a time; and one clergyperson and consecrated religious at a time, he converted others by being an example of conversion. It worked from the bottom up. And it reached all the way to the top of the church. This is still possible today! When people change, nations can change. Then the entire world can change. This is what happened with Francis in the thirteenth century as Europe was "carpeted with friars," as Dante said. A warring Europe was pacified, and a peace movement spread in a whole new way. It can spread in our day as well!

These Admonitions require a complete letting go of the old self through the cross of Jesus Christ, being born again by the Spirit of God, and being raised up a new person in Christ.

Learning these lessons requires a complete letting go of old habits and patterns on both a personal and cultural level. They call for real, radical change to the core of who we are.

I pray that this book has helped you see this new way in Christ that is rooted so deeply in an ancient past. It worked for the greatest saints. It can also work for us if we dare to receive it.

About Paraclete Press

WHO WE ARE

As the publishing arm of the Community of Jesus, Paraclete Press presents a full expression of Christian belief and practice—from Catholic to Evangelical, from Protestant to Orthodox, reflecting the ecumenical charism of the Community and its dedication to sacred music, the fine arts, and the written word. We publish books, recordings, sheet music, and video/DVDs that nourish the vibrant life of the church and its people.

WHAT WE ARE DOING

BOOKS | PARACLETE PRESS BOOKS show the richness and depth of what it means to be Christian. While Benedictine spirituality is at the heart of who we are and all that we do, our books reflect the Christian experience across many cultures, time periods, and houses of worship.

We have many series, including *Paraclete Essentials*; *Paraclete Fiction*; *Paraclete Poetry*; *Paraclete Giants*; and for children and adults, *All God's Creatures*, books about animals and faith; and *San Damiano Books*, focusing on Franciscan spirituality. Others include *Voices from the Monastery* (men and women monastics writing about living a spiritual life today), *Active Prayer*, and new for young readers: *The Pope's Cat*. We also specialize in gift books for children on the occasions of Baptism and First Communion, as well as other important times in a child's life, and books that bring creativity and liveliness to any adult spiritual life.

The MOUNT TABOR BOOKS series focuses on the arts and literature as well as liturgical worship and spirituality; it was created in conjunction with the Mount Tabor Ecumenical Centre for Art and Spirituality in Barga, Italy.

MUSIC | The PARACLETE RECORDINGS label represents the internationally acclaimed choir *Gloriæ Dei Cantores*, the *Gloriæ Dei Cantores Schola*, and the other instrumental artists of the *Arts Empowering Life Foundation*.

Paraclete Press is the exclusive North American distributor for the Gregorian chant recordings from St. Peter's Abbey in Solesmes, France. Paraclete also carries all of the Solesmes chant publications for Mass and the Divine Office, as well as their academic research publications.

In addition, PARACLETE PRESS SHEET MUSIC publishes the work of today's finest composers of sacred choral music, annually reviewing over 1,000 works and releasing between 40 and 60 works for both choir and organ.

VIDEO | Our video/DVDs offer spiritual help, healing, and biblical guidance for a broad range of life issues including grief and loss, marriage, forgiveness, facing death, understanding suicide, bullying, addictions, Alzheimer's, and Christian formation.

Learn more about us at our website:
www.paracletepress.com
or phone us toll-free at 1.800.451.5006

SCAN
TO
READ
MORE

You may also be interested in . . .

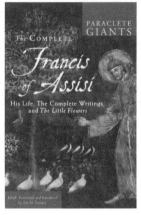

The Complete Francis of Assisi
His Life, The Complete Writings, and The Little Flowers

Edited, Translated, and Introduced by Jon M. Sweeney

ISBN 978-1-61261-688-9 | $29.99 | Trade paper

Francis of Assisi in His Own Words
The Essential Writings – Second Edition

Translated and Annotated by Jon M. Sweeney

ISBN 978-1-64060-019-5 | $16.99 | Trade paper

The St. Francis Prayer Book
A Guide to Deepen Your Spiritual Life

Jon M. Sweeney

ISBN 978-1-55725-352-1 | $16.99 | Trade paper

Available at bookstores
Paraclete Press | 1-800-451-5006
www.paracletepress.com